Instructions to Beginners
In the Christian Life

Instructions to Beginners
in the
Christian Life

Prepared by a Committee
Appointed by the Southwestern Pennsylvania
(Now Allegheny)
Mennonite Conference

John L. Horst, Editor

William C. Hershberger

Joseph M. Nissley

HERALD PRESS
Scottdale, Pennsylvania
Waterloo, Ontario

The paper used in this publication is recycled and meets
the minimum requirements of American National Standard
for Information Sciences—Permanence of Paper for Printed
Library Materials, ANSI Z39.48-1984.

INSTRUCTIONS TO BEGINNERS
IN THE CHRISTIAN LIFE
Published since 1934 by Herald Press, Scottdale, Pa. 15683
 Released simultaneously in Canada by Herald Press,
 Waterloo, Ont. N2L 6H7. All rights reserved.
International Standard Book Number: 0-8361-1378-0
Printed in the United States of America

99 98 97 96 95 94   28 27 26 25 24 23

PREFACE

For some time past brethren in different quarters of the Church felt that there was need of more uniformity, in subject matter used and methods followed, in the instruction of applicants for church membership. Some of our brethren were so impressed with this need that they brought the matter before the Southwestern Pennsylvania Church Conference, which in regular annual session at the Weaver Church, near Johnstown, Pa., Aug. 14, 15, 1930, adopted the following recommendations: "We recommend that a booklet be prepared with a view to unifying the subject matter to be used in the instruction of applicants for church membership. We suggest that the booklet be submitted to the Publication Board for publication in the regular manner. For the carrying out of this recommendation we suggest the following committee: John L. Horst, W. C. Hershberger, and J. M. Nissley."

Some time after their appointment the committee met and made plans for carrying out the work that was thus assigned to them. It was decided that the book should not be too large and yet include a comprehensive statement of Christian doctrines, ordinances, and principles, giving outlines with Scripture references, practical comments, and questions upon the subjects treated. This plan has been followed throughout the book with a few modifications. It has been the aim to treat the subjects as briefly as possible, consistent with giving the information that it was thought most important for the applicant for church membership to have.

Considerable time and labor were put into the work of preparing the material for this little book. Numerous works on the subjects treated were consulted, and the manuscript was submitted to the Publishing Committee of the Mennonite Publication Board for criticism and approval. For all the help received from these sources we wish to give recognition and to tender our thanks. We trust that the finished book may, under the blessing of God, at least in a measure meet the need which it was designed to supply. And as we send it forth on its mission we pray that the Lord may bless it to the building up of His Church here below.

The Committee.

PUBLISHER'S PREFACE

We are grateful to God and to our constituency for the way in which this little book has been received and used by those in the church whose duty and privilege it is to lead beginners in the Christian life into the fullness of blessing which every Christian should enjoy. With the exception of a few changes which were made for the second printing, this printing is the same as the first. May the Lord continue to bless and use this little volume in building up believers in Christ and thus to the honor and glory of God.

The Publisher.

TABLE OF CONTENTS

INTRODUCTORY

The Contents of This Book

The Table of Contents will at a glance give an idea of the scope of material found in this book. It was thought best to begin with the plan of salvation, stating some of the most important points concerning both God's part and man's part, so that the convert may have a good foundation upon which to build his Christian life. Unless these fundamentals are grasped it will be hard to lead the young disciple into a definite assurance of salvation and an appreciation of the doctrines of the Church and the principles of the Christian life. He should at once begin to build up his spiritual life by prayer and Bible reading and have the assurance of the presence of the Holy Spirit in his life. Then with a heart given to Christ in full consecration and whole-hearted dedication to His service, he will be in a position to appreciate and understand the ordinances and doctrines of the Church.

The ordinances are given careful treatment in one chapter and some of the great doctrines, principles, and restrictions in another. Then follow in briefer form some of the most important matters concerning Christian life and conduct and the need of witnessing for Jesus through the activities of the Church. The main part of the book closes with a few thoughts concerning the blessings and rewards of the Christian life, leading the beginner in the Christian life to look forward to the incomprehensible blessings and glories that await the faithful in the world to come. The last chapter, "The Administration of Baptism," is taken from the "Minister's Manual." Because of its helpful instructions it was thought wise to include it in this book.

How to Use This Book

The material of the book is arranged with the idea in mind of having about seven meetings of instruction. There are seven main chapters, but these are not of equal length. In the beginning of the book it may not be possible to cover every chapter in one meeting. In that case, as for instance in the Chapter on Church Membership and Christian Ordinances, two or more meetings may be devoted to one chapter. Toward the close of the book, where the chapters are shorter, two or more chapters may be covered in one meeting, if the time is limited. It was the aim of the compilers of the book to give the largest amount of material on the doctrines and ordinances of the Church and the most important principles of the Christian life. The one in charge of the instruction meetings should use his own judgment as to how much time he will spend upon the various chapters. In this he must take into consideration the greatest needs of the particular class with which he is dealing. If he is located in a mission station where the applicants are not very familiar with the teachings of the Bible and the rules and regulations of the Church he will naturally spend more time in instructing the class than in a congregation where the applicants are quite familiar with our beliefs and practices. In no case, however, should careless or inadequate instruction be given. All applicants need to be instructed sufficiently to give them a thorough grasp of the plan of salvation, the ordinances and doctrines of the Church, and the principles of the Christian life.

It is the aim of those who prepared this book to present an abundance of material in a brief, comprehensive form, so that the instructor might choose from the matter presented just what he felt the particular class of applicants needed most. It is even possible to cover the material in the book in three or four meetings, if the person in charge of the instruction selects only the material that he feels it is most necessary to give.

The material on the different subjects in the greater part of the book is presented in three parts: Outline with Scripture References, Practical Comments, and Questions. In many of the subjects quite a number of Scripture references are given. These may be given out to the class, and, after being read, used as the basis for discussion. In many cases there may not be time to read all the references, in which case only a selected number of them may be given. The comments are based directly upon the outline and are designed to give the instructor some ideas as to how the subjects may be handled. In most of the chapters questions on the subject are also given. These may or may not be used, according to the discretion of the instructor. They may be valuable for review of past chapters, when the leader begins a new chapter at the next meeting.

The book is designed to serve a dual purpose: first, as a guide to the instructor, both in furnishing material to be used and the method of presenting it; second, as a book to be read and studied by the convert. If the book is given to the applicant he may be instructed to look up the references on the subjects to be discussed at the next meeting. This will put him into a better position to receive the instructions given by the minister.

Finally, the book is intended to be a help and a guide; not something that must be followed in every detail. It will depend much upon the instructor as to how thoroughly the doctrines and principles of the Church are implanted into the heart and mind of the applicant.

Instruction Meetings

Methods of holding these meetings vary in different localities. Sometimes the meetings are held just prior to the church services in one of the smaller rooms in the church building. In other cases the

meetings are held on Sunday afternoons or on week-
day evenings. Sometimes the meetings are largely
private, with only the ministers and converts present,
at other times most of the congregation may be in
attendance. Some find it profitable to have the instruction meetings at the time of the regular midweek
prayer meetings. All of these methods may be good,
and it remains for the church leaders to choose
the form best adapted to meet the needs of the people
with whom they are working. Sometimes the instruction is carried on over a long period of time; at other
times only brief instructions are given. The meetings
should be held often enough to present such an in-
clusive scope of material that the applicant will be well
grounded in the principles of the faith and the doctrines and practices of the Church. See the last chapter entitled "Administration of Baptism."

Custom also varies as to who does the instructing.
Sometimes this work is taken care of largely by the
bishop, at other times by the home ministers, and in
some cases when revival meetings are in progress the
evangelist holds instruction meetings in connection
with the regular services.

Other books and pamphlets that will be helpful
for use by the leader of the instruction meetings are:
"Doctrines of the Bible"; "One Thousand Questions
and Answers on Points of Christian Doctrine"; "Confession of Faith and Minister's Manual"; "The Way
of Salvation"; "God's Plan of Salvation"; "Junior
Catechism"; "A Lighthouse for Young Believers"; "A

Letter to Young Church Members"; and the pocket edition of "Confession of Faith." All of these may be obtained from the publishers of this book. At some time during the instructions the Rules and Discipline of the Church Conference should be explained to the applicants.

Personal Interviews

No instructions to converts should be considered complete until the ministry has had private personal interviews with each applicant, so that personal experiences and problems may be discussed and individual help may be given wherever it is needed. Assistance may be given in specific cases in this way which could never be supplied in the general instruction meeting.

Chapter One

THE PLAN OF SALVATION

We begin this series of instructions with the plan of salvation because we feel that every one who takes a stand for Christ should have a clear understanding of what this step means and have a firm foundation upon which to build his future Christian life. God's plan of salvation was conceived through the wisdom of an infinite mind, and we may never be able on this earth to fathom the depths of its meaning. Yet it is simple enough so that every one who has a sound mind can grasp its teachings to such an extent as to be able to find salvation. Opinions vary as to how the subjects embraced in the plan of salvation should be treated or in what form they should be arranged. If we get the main principles it may not matter so much in what order we study them, but we should remember that from beginning to end salvation is the work of God, and that even the part which man must do could never be accomplished but by the grace and goodness of God. We have tried to keep the material in a simple form and shall discuss it under these four heads: Sin; The Saviour from Sin; Man's Part in the Plan of Salvation; and Assurance and Continuance.

I. SIN

Outline Study*

1. Original state of man.—Gen. 1:26, 27.
2. Origin of sin.—Gen. 3:1-6.
3. Some definitions of sin:
    a. Trangression.—I Jno. 3:4.
    b. Unrighteousness.—I Jno. 5:17.
    c. Unbelief.—Rom. 14:23.
    d. Neglect.—Jas. 4:17.
    e. Foolishness.—Prov. 24:9.
4. Result of sin—death.—Gen. 2:17; Rom. 5:12, 14, 19; 6:23; Ezek. 18:4.
5. Our sinful condition by nature.—Gen. 6:5, 12; Psa. 51:5; Jer. 17:9; Isa. 64:6; 53:6; Rom. 3:23; Eph. 2:1, 2; I Jno. 1:8.

Practical Comments

In the beginning, when God created all things, He crowned His work by making man in His own image. Man was created innocent, pure, and sinless. Man is different from the animals in this that he was

---

* In these Outline Studies, especially the more lengthy ones, there may be more Scripture references than can be read and discussed in the meeting. In that case only such as the instructor may select should be given. However, it will be well to have the applicants look up all the references in their home study. See page 10 in the Introduction for further instruction as to how to use the book.

created in the image of God and has within him an eternal principle with which no other creature is endowed. Sin had its origin, as far as man is concerned, when Satan, in the guise of a serpent, tempted our first parents, and they yielded and partook of the forbidden fruit. This brings us to the definitions of sin, as given above. God had given His law that they should not eat of the fruit of "the tree of the knowledge of good and evil," and when Adam and Eve did so they transgressed that law—they had now sinned. The sins of unrighteousness, unbelief, and neglect all entered in here, and probably also that of foolishness, for it is the height of foolishness to listen to Satan and disobey God.

The result of this sin was that both natural and spiritual death passed upon our first parents. The seeds of natural death immediately took root in the bodies of Adam and Eve, and they became subject to physical death, which before the advent of sin was not the case. Spiritual death, separation from God, took place at once. Through Adam, then, the head of the race, death passed upon the whole human family, and now all of us, as descendants of Adam and Eve, are subject to death. The effect of Adam's sin was such that his nature was changed from a state of innocency to that of sin. The trait or character of asserting himself against the Father's will was transmitted to his children and thus to all the human race. Thus all of us are sinners by nature. None are righteous; we have all gone astray from God. This sinful nature is

apparent even in small children and becomes more so
as they grow older. They are, however, not responsible
until they are old enough to know right from wrong.
Unless people see their own sinfulness they will not
appreciate their need of a Saviour.

Questions

What was man's original state when God created him?
How did sin begin, as far as man is concerned?
Give some Bible definitions of sin.
How did sin affect our first parents?
How did the fall of man affect us?
Are all people sinners?

II. THE SAVIOUR FROM SIN

Outline Study

1. God provided a Saviour from sin.—Matt. 1:21;
   Luke 1:31; 19:10; Jno. 3:16, 17; I Tim. 1:15; Heb.
   7:25.

2. He is our Substitute.—Isa. 53:5; II Cor. 5:21; Gal.
   3:13; Heb. 2:9; I Pet. 3:18.

3. He is our Sacrifice for sin.—Jno. 1:29; Isa. 53:7; I
   Pet. 1:19.

4. How we receive salvation by faith in His atoning
   work.—Jno. 3:16; 1:12; 5:24; 11:25; Acts 16:31;
   Rom. 10:9; Heb. 11:6.

Practical Comments

In our discussion of sin we learned that every one is born in sin and that we by nature are, in the sight of God, vile sinners whose righteousnesses are as filthy rags. We are now ready to consider how God has provided a way by which every one may be saved. He is a righteous God, and His justice demands that every person should suffer the penalty of death which He has pronounced upon the sinner. Man as a rebel against God was entirely helpless to save himself. But God in His great mercy loved even sinful man so much that He provided a Saviour for him in the person of His only begotten Son. God sent His Son Jesus into the world for no other reason than to become the Saviour of all mankind. He came to seek and to save the lost. Justice and mercy were combined in God's plan of salvation. Jesus, who was altogether holy and righteous, gave His life as a ransom for our sins. He became our Substitute and bore, in our stead, the death penalty which we deserved. Thus, through Jesus' death on the cross, every sinner was set free, or delivered from the bondage of sin and death. In Old Testament times animals were sacrificed as sin offerings. Jesus Christ, as the Lamb of God, was the fulfillment of these Old Testament sacrifices, redeeming us by His own precious blood which was shed upon the cross.

All of the foregoing was included in God's part in providing salvation for sinful man. Jesus tasted death for every man, but how is man to receive salvation and have the assurance that he is a child of God? Salvation is only made available to individual persons as they by faith accept Jesus as their Saviour. The references given above show very conclusively that only as we believe on Him can we be saved and become the children of God. If we believe with all our hearts that Jesus is the Son of God and our Saviour from sin we may have the definite assurance that our sins are forgiven and that we are children of God.

Questions

How could a holy God provide a way of salvation to sinful man?

In what way was a Saviour provided, historically speaking?

How could sinful man escape the death penalty which he deserved and which God had pronounced upon sin?

If Jesus died for the sins of the whole world why are not all people saved?

How is the atoning work of Christ made available to us as individuals?

How do we accept the pardon for our sins which Jesus wrought on the cross?

III. MAN'S PART IN THE PLAN OF SALVATION AND THE RESULTS

Outline Study

1. Repentance, or sorrow for sin and change of purpose.—Matt. 3:2; 4:17; Luke 13:3, 5; 24:47; Acts 2:38; 17:30; 20:21; 26:20; II Pet. 3:9.
2. Restitution.—Ex. 22:2-4; Lev. 6:4; Prov. 6:30, 31; Ezek. 33:14, 15; Luke 19:8; Acts 3:21.
3. Confession:
   a. Confession of Christ.—Matt. 10:32; Luke 12:8; Rom. 10:9; I Jno. 4:15; Matt. 16:16.
   b. Confession of sin.—I Jno. 1:9; Prov. 28:13; Jas. 5:16.
4. Conversion, a change of heart and life, the result of accepting God's plan of salvation.
   a. Its importance.—Matt. 18:3; Acts 3:19.
   b. Instruments through which conversion is accomplished.—Psa. 19:7; 51:13; Jas. 5:19, 20.
   c. Result, changed creatures, a new life.—Jno. 1: 12, 13; 3:3, 5; II Cor. 5:17.

Practical Comments

Repentance is one of the absolutely essential conditions of salvation. Repentance is a godly sorrow for sin that causes a person not only to grieve because of the wrong committed but to have such a hatred for sin that he firmly determines to forsake it. John the Baptist preached repentance, Jesus declared it to be essential to salvation, and the apostles in the early Church did the same. We must not minimize its importance. It matters not so much which comes first, faith or repentance, but both are conditions which we must meet in order to obtain salvation.

Another necessary condition in properly beginning the Christian life is that of making restitution for wrongs done to other people. This principle is strongly emphasized in the Old Testament, and it is reaffirmed in the New Testament. A spirit of true repentance manifests itself in a willingness to make wrong things right, as by restoring any property that may have been wrongfully obtained and correcting any false statements that have been injurious to others. Many people make a bad beginning in the Christian life and fail to get assurance that they are saved because they do not meet the condition of restitution.

Another most important condition is that of confession. This has several meanings. First is that of openly confessing Christ before our fellow men. On this point God gives us some very precious promises, as the above Scripture references show. Let us meet the conditions, and then we can unhesitatingly claim these promises as applying to ourselves. Then there is the matter of confessing our sins. We should do this first to God, telling Him of our sins and that we are sorry for having committed them. Then we should confess our sins to our fellow men as far as we have done things to injure them. This is closely coupled with restitution.

Conversion is a change of heart which God gives us through the new birth when we meet the conditions that He has given in His Word. We are then born again, are made new creatures in Christ Jesus, and are His spiritual children.

On God's part in salvation we have the regeneration of the heart and life; on man's part we have the surrender of the will and the life so that He can make us new creatures. But all the conditions that He lays down for us can only be met through His grace and the operation of His Spirit in our hearts. The goodness of God leads us to repentance. Rom. 2:4.

Questions

Give a definition of repentance.

How many kinds of repentance are there? II Cor. 7:10.

Is repentance absolutely essential to salvation?

What blessings do we receive through restitution?

How many kinds of confession are taught in the Bible in connection with the plan of salvation? Explain.

Explain God's part and man's part in conversion.

To whom belong all the glory and praise in the matter of salvation?

IV.   ASSURANCE AND CONTINUANCE

Outline Study

1. It is possible for us to know that we are saved.— I Jno. 5:13.

2. The threefold basis of assurance:
   a. The Word.—I Thess. 1:5; I Jno. 5:13; Jno. 1:
      12; 3:36; Acts 13:39.
   b. The Life.—I Jno. 3:14; 4:7, 16; 5:10.
   c. The Spirit.—Rom. 8:14-17.
3. Phases of assurance:
   a. Understanding.—Col. 2:2, 3.
   b. Faith.—Heb. 10:22.
   c. Love.—I Jno. 3:18, 19.
   d. Hope.—Heb. 6:11.
4. The importance of continuing in the Christian life
   —Jno. 8:31; 15:2-6; I Jno. 2:24.
5. God will keep us if we give ourselves into His
   hands.—I Pet. 1:4, 5; Jude 24, 25.

Practical Comments

It is possible for beginners in the Christian life to
know that their sins are forgiven and that they are
children of God. According to I Jno. 5:13 the purpose
of this epistle is that believers might be assured that
they are children of God and have eternal life. If we
have met the conditions for salvation as set forth in
God's Word, we may then find assurance by resting
in faith upon the promises of God. If we have actually
believed on Jesus Christ as our Saviour, have repented
of our sins, and have accepted Him as our Lord and
Master we need have no doubt that we are His sons
and daughters. We have a further witness in our
own lives. If we see that our lives have been changed

and that we have a fervent love for the brethren and for God, who is the Giver of this love, we may rest assured that we have been born again and are the children of God. In that case the Spirit of God will dwell in our hearts and will also give us the witness that we are children of God and joint-heirs with Jesus Christ. This assurance will give us joy and peace in our hearts and will lead us to a fuller understanding of God's Word and to new heights of faith, love, and hope. In this connection it is well to remember that it is now our duty to continue in the faith and life which we have begun, committing our all to Him who is able to keep us until the end. I Tim. 1:12.

Questions

Is it possible for us to have the assurance that we are saved and are the children of God?

Through what means does this assurance come?

Can we have such assurance if we have not complied with all the conditions which God gives in His Word as necessary in order to be adopted as children of God?

Having met those conditions, is there any reason why we should doubt our acceptance and position as God's children?

What will this assurance bring us?

Why is it important to continue in the new life which we have begun?

Chapter Two

BEGINNING THE CHRISTIAN LIFE

It is a fine thing to begin the Christian life. The decision to do so is the wisest and noblest that anyone can make. And it is of the utmost importance that we begin right. Failing to do so may lead to disaster, for many people who stand for Christ never make any real headway in the Christian life. A clear understanding of the plan of salvation as outlined in the previous chapter will help us to get a firm foundation for our faith and an assurance that we have forsaken our sins, have turned to God, and have become His children. But now that we are newborn children in the kingdom or family of God we should grow and develop in the Christian life, just as we expect children to develop physically and mentally in the natural life. In II Pet. 3:18 we read: "But grow in grace, and in the knowledge of our Lord and Saviour Jesus Christ." Paul speaks of those who failed to develop in the Christian life as they should have, in these words: "And I, brethren, could not speak unto you as unto spiritual, but as unto carnal, even as unto babes in Christ" (I Cor. 3:1). We must begin as babes, but we should not continue in that state; we should make a normal, healthy growth in the Christian life. In this chapter we shall consider the following aids to spiritual growth: Bible Reading; Prayer; The Infilling of the Holy Spirit; Consecration; Service.

I. BIBLE READING

Outline Study

1. Names which show what the Bible is:
   a. The Word of God.—Heb. 4:12; I Pet. 1:23.
   b. The Holy Scriptures.—II Tim. 3:15; II Pet. 3:16.
   c. The Law of the Lord.—Psa. 1:2; 19:17.
2. How it was given:
   a. By inspiration of God.—II Tim. 3:16.
   b. Through holy men, speaking by the Holy Ghost.—II Pet. 1:21.
   c. Proofs of inspiration—its inerrancy, its unity, the minute fulfillment of its prophecies, its effect upon people's lives, its centering upon Christ, its own claims.
3. Purpose of the Bible:
   a. To show the way of life.—Jno. 5:39; 6:63.
   b. To give light.—Psa. 119:105.
   c. To keep from sin and its consequences.—Psa. 19:11; 119:11.
4. What the Bible does for us when its message is heeded:
   a. We are born again.—I Pet. 1:23-25.
   b. We are cleansed.—Psa. 119:9; Jno. 15:3.
   c. We grow.—I Pet. 2:2.
   d. We are protected and defended.—Eph. 6:17.

Practical Comments

One of the most important things for the young Christian to attain is an established belief that the Bible is the Word of God, in which is revealed the will of God for man, and that this revelation is without error of any kind. We should settle in our minds, once for all, that the Bible is different from all other books in this that it was given by inspiration of God. Thirty-six different authors wrote sixty-six books over a period of sixteen centuries, and yet they agree in everything which they teach. This can be accounted for only on the ground that the Holy Ghost directed the authors what to write and kept them from all error. The accurate way in which the prophecies of the Old Testament were fulfilled shows that the Bible is more than a human book. It is said that there are three hundred thirty minute details predicted concerning the life of Christ, every one of which came true.

Through the teachings of the Bible the lives of many people have been transformed, the vilest of sinners becoming saints of God. If we allow its message to have its way in our hearts it will save us from sin and make us new creatures in Christ. It also shows us how to live for Christ and how to serve Him acceptably. "Its doctrines are holy, its precepts are binding, its histories are true, its decisions are immutable. Read it to be wise, believe it to be safe, and practice it to be holy. It contains light to direct you, food to support you, and comfort to cheer you." The Bible very emphatically claims to be the Word of God. We accept this statement as true along with its other teachings.

One of the things that will greatly aid a person to grow and develop in the Christian life is regular, daily reading of the Bible. A good way to begin is to read the Gospel of John. It is perhaps the clearest in its statement of the plan of salvation. Then read the other Gospels and the Acts and continue on through the New Testament. It may be best to read the New Testament through a number of times in order to get familiar with its message. After this the young Christian should read the Old Testament also. Begin with Genesis and read on through. Two chapters daily from the Old Testament and one from the New Testament will make a fine reading schedule. Three chapters every week day and five every Sunday will take one through the entire Bible in a year's time. In connection with his daily devotional Bible reading the convert should study his Sunday-school lesson well, attend prayer meetings, preaching services, and young people's Bible meetings and use every opportunity to become familiar with God's Word. Then he should meditate upon its teachings and put them to practice in his daily life.

Questions

What names are applied to the Bible?
How do we know that the Bible is God's Word?
In what ways is it different from other books?
What is the purpose of the Bible?

What are some of the things it does for us?
Name some good ways of studying the Bible.

II. PRAYER

Outline Study

1. Prayer is the term used when a child of God talks
   to the heavenly Father.—Rom. 8:15; Gal. 4:6.
2. It is a command of God.—Luke 18:1; 21:36; I
   Thess. 5:17.
3. Phases of prayer:
   a. Asking.—Matt. 7:7.
   b. Thanksgiving.—Phil. 4:6.
   c. Praise.—Heb. 13:15.
   d. Intercession.—I Tim. 2:1, 2.
4. Kinds of prayer:
   a. Private.—Matt. 6:5, 6.
   b. Public.—Jno. 11:41, 42.
5. Times to pray.—Psa. 55:16, 17; Dan. 6:10; Mark
   1:35; Luke 6:12; Matt. 14:19; Acts 27:35; Eph.
   6:18; I Thess. 5:17.
6. For whom and what to pray:
   a. All men, especially rulers.—I Tim. 2:1-4.
   b. Unsaved.—Rom. 10:1.
   c. One another.—Jas. 5:16.
   d. Ministers, teachers, and Christian workers.—
      I Thess. 3:1, 2; Matt. 9:38.
   e. All saints.—Eph. 6:18, 19.
   f. Enemies.—Matt. 5:44.

g. Ourselves.—II Cor. 12:7, 8.

h. Wisdom.—Jas. 1:5.

i. Cleansing.—Psa. 51:7.

j. To be kept from temptation.—Matt. 6:13; Luke 22:40.

k. All things.—Matt. 21:22.

7. How to pray:

a. In the name of Christ.—Jno. 14:13, 14; 15:16.

b. According to God's will.—I Jno. 5:14.

c. In faith.—Matt. 21:22.

d. With importunity or perseverance.—Luke 18: 1-8.

8. Hindrances to prayer:

a. Sin.—Isa. 59:2; Psa. 66:18.

b. Selfishness.—Jas. 4:3.

c. An unforgiving spirit.—Mark 11:25, 26.

9. Promises of answered prayer.—Psa. 91:15; Isa. 58:9; 65:24; Luke 11:9; Jno. 15:7.

Practical Comments

Just as it is necessary that we read the Bible and have God talk to us, so it is necessary that we pray or talk to God. It should be just as natural for a child of God to talk to the heavenly Father as it is for an earthly child to talk to its parents and make its wishes known. At the same time it is well for us to remember that we are commanded to pray. Jesus, however, in His discourses usually takes it for granted that His followers should pray. While we are told to make our requests known to God, we should remember there is more to prayer than asking favors for ourselves. Prayer should have in it the elements of thanksgiving and praise to God and intercession in behalf of others.

We should learn to pray both in private and in public, and have regular seasons for private devotion. Remember that the great men of God have been men who spent much time in prayer. Early morning hours are fine for devotion. We should pray at all times, but especially before important events. A help in prayer life is to make a list of people and things to pray for. But we can not expect God to hear our prayers if we live lives of sin or ask selfishly for things to advance our own personal interests. We should guard against all wrong motives when we pray. But if we ask according to the will of God, under the direction of His Spirit, for His glory, and in the name of His Son, He has promised to hear and answer our prayers. The young convert should especially make it a rule to give thanks at mealtimes, to pray before retiring, and to ask God's blessing and guidance at the beginning of each new day. If we give ourselves definitely into God's care each day we will have gone a long way in successfully meeting the temptations and trials that may come to us, as well as in fitting ourselves for the duties that God has for us to perform. Sisters should wear their devotional coverings during prayer. This ordinance will be explained later.

Questions

Give a definition of prayer.

Why should we pray?

What are some of the different phases of prayer?

Name some different kinds of prayer.

State some appropriate times for prayer.

Should we be prepared to pray at all times?

Give a list of persons and things we should pray for.

Name some conditions of successful prayer. Some hindrances.

How do we know that the Lord hears and answers prayer?

III. THE HOLY SPIRIT

Outline Study

1. The Holy Spirit is a person. Personal pronouns are used in speaking of Him.—Jno. 14:16, 17; 15:26.
2. He is one of the three persons of the Holy Trinity. Matt. 28:19, 20; II Cor. 13:14.
3. He is spoken of as God.—Acts 5:3, 4; I Cor. 3:16.
4. He has Divine attributes:
   a. Eternity.—Heb. 9:14.
   b. Holiness.—Eph. 4:30.
   c. Omnipresence, everywhere present.—Psa. 139:7-10.
   d. Omniscience, all knowing.—I Cor. 2:10, 11.
5. His work:
   a. Convicts of sin.—Jno. 16:8.
   b. Regenerates the heart.—Jno. 3:5.

    c. Indwells the believer.—Jno. 14:7; Rom. 8:9.

    d. Gives assurance.—Rom. 8:14-17.

    e. Guides the believer.—Jno. 16:13; Acts 8:39; 10:19, 20; 16:6.

    f. Calls to and empowers for service.—Acts 13:2; 1:8.

    g. Comforts the believer.—Jno. 14:16-18.

    h. Teaches the believer.—Jno. 14:26.

    i. Testifies of Christ.—Jno. 15:26, 27.

6. Fruit of the Spirit.—Gal. 5:22, 23; Jno. 15:16.

7. Conditions for receiving the Spirit:

    a. Repentance and faith.—Acts 2:38.

    b. Obedience.—Acts 5:32.

    c. Asking.—Luke 11:13.

    d. Abiding in Christ.—Jno. 15:4, 5.

8. There is a continual conflict between the flesh and the Spirit.—Rom. 8; Gal. 5:16-26.

9. We should yield to the Spirit.—Rom. 6:13; Eph. 4:30; I Thess. 5:19.

Practical Comments

When Jesus was about to leave His disciples on earth and return to the Father in heaven He gave them the definite promise that He would send them a Comforter to teach and guide and help them in His absence. This was the Holy Spirit, who came upon the disciples in visible form on the day of Pentecost. He is a real person, not merely an influence, and is one of the three members of the Godhead. He is eternal, having always been with the Father, and has from the beginning performed His particular sphere of work. In the case of the sinner He brings conviction of sin, and when the sinner yields He has a definite work to do in his regeneration and conversion. He has a great work to perform in connection with the life of the believer, and every beginner in the Christian life should have the Holy Spirit dwelling within his heart to give assurance that he is really a child of God, to teach him the things of God, and to lead him into all truth.

The Holy Spirit inspired the Scriptures (II Pet. 1:21), and He is the best Teacher and Interpreter of them. It is part of His work to call the believer into definite fields of service and to guide and direct him in the work of the Lord. He gives the power to make that service effective to the salvation of souls and the building up of the Church. He comforts the believer in the trials and conflicts of life and helps him to testify of the Christ who saved him from a life of sin. He also moulds the life of the believer so that the beautiful traits of character as recorded in Gal. 5:22, 23 are developed. Thus He produces a well-balanced, beautiful Christian life which is a glory to God and a benediction to fellow men.

It is important that every believer should know the conditions that God in His Word has laid down as necessary to be complied with in order to receive the Spirit. Having met those conditions, the Christian should then believe that he has the Holy Spirit, as God has promised that he should have, and fully yield to

His guidance and leading. The flesh and the Spirit are opposed to each other. We have that dual nature, as Christians, and we must learn to yield to and walk in the Spirit so that we do not give way to the lusts of the flesh. A Spirit-filled life is a successful, victorious Christian life.

Questions

Give some proofs that the Holy Spirit is a person.

What relation is He to the Holy Trinity?

What is His work with regard to the sinner?

What is His work in the life of the believer?

Enumerate the fruit of the Spirit.

What are the conditions that we must meet in order to be assured that we have the abiding presence of the Holy Spirit in our lives?

Is it possible for us to know that we have the Holy Spirit?

Why is it important that we yield our lives to the direction of the Spirit?

IV. CONSECRATION

Outline Study

1. Consecration means to offer or devote anything to the service or worship of God.—I Chron. 29:5.
2. Examples of consecration:
   a. Abraham offering Isaac.—Gen. 22.
   b. First-born.—Ex. 13:2, 12, 15.

    c. Levites.—Num. 3:12, 13.

    d. Hannah giving Samuel.—I Sam. 1:11, 27, 28.

3. The reasonableness of consecration.—Rom. 12:1;
    I Chron. 29:11-14.

4. The joy of consecration.—I Chron. 29:9, 17.

5. The call to consecration.—Ex. 32:29; Prov. 23:26;
    I Chron. 28:9; I Cor. 10:31.

6. The secret of consecration.—II Cor. 5:14, 15; I Jno.
    4:19.

7. Christ, our Example in consecration.—Heb. 7:28.

Practical Comments

The Christian convert should at once face the question of full consecration to the service of God. Just as Abraham gave Isaac, or as Hannah gave Samuel, wholly to the service of God, so each one who begins the Christian life should give himself fully to God to be used in any way that He may choose. This does not mean that the young Christian should drop his ordinary duties of home, school, farm, shop, or business, unless such are actually sinful in their nature. But there is this change. As Christians we now do these things for the Master, keeping in mind the glory of God and not the desires of the flesh. Christ is enthroned in the life, and self and Satan are deposed. To give ourselves thus wholly to God is a most reasonable thing to do because of what He has done for us, both in creation and in our redemption through the Lord Jesus Christ. This full surrender is what brings real joy and peace to the Christian. Failing to do that his Christian life seems a burden and service a drudgery.

The call to consecration comes to every one, and it is the crying need of the Church today. Let us dedicate to God our time, talents, substance, and lives. Christ is our supreme Example. He devoted Himself entirely to doing the will of the Lord. That was the purpose for which He came into the world. He carried out that purpose, and even today He, as our High Priest, is still doing the work for which He was consecrated. The secret of the consecrated life is a love for Christ and His Church and a willingness to serve in any capacity to which He may call us.

Questions

What is the meaning of consecration?

What Bible examples can you give?

Why should every Christian consecrate himself fully to the Lord?

How does consecration affect our everyday life and conduct?

Does the call for consecration come to every Christian?

Who is our perfect Example?

V. SERVICE

Outline Study

1. The call to service.—Deut. 10:12; Matt. 4:19; Eph. 6:7; Heb. 12:28; Col. 3:22-25; I Cor. 7:22; Mark 13:34; Eph. 2:10.
2. The need of service or spiritual exercise.—I Tim. 4:7, 8.
3. Forms of service.—Jno. 12:3, 26; Gal. 6:2; Mark 10:43; Matt. 10:22; Acts 20:18, 19; 9:20; Jno. 13:14; I Tim. 6:18; Matt. 25:34-40; 9:37, 38; Jno. 4:35, 36.
4. The joy of service.—Psa. 126:5, 6; Luke 10:17; Jno. 4:36; Matt. 25:21, 34.
5. Christ our Example in service.—Matt. 20:28; Luke 22:27; Jno. 13:4, 5; Phil. 2:7.

Practical Comments

To every one who has heard the call of Christ to salvation comes also the call to service. It is but natural that the person who has given himself to the Lord in full consecration should, like the Apostle Paul, ask the question, "Lord, what wilt thou have me to do?" There is an abundance of Scripture teaching to show that we are saved to serve. Christ needs our service, for He carries on His work through human instrumentalities. But we need this service also. Just as a natural child cannot be expected to make a healthy growth of body or mind without exercise, neither can the child of God grow spiritually without exercise or service in the Christian life. And only as we begin at once thus to exercise ourselves and continue to do so, can we hope to make progress in a spiritual way.

There are many forms of this service or exercise. First, there is direct service for Christ—prayer, testimony, praise, and speaking for Him in private and public whenever we have opportunity. Then may be mentioned service to our fellow man, which, if done in the right spirit, is accounted by the Master as being done unto Him. There is also the service of clean, upright living, shining for Jesus wherever we are. The Church will open up many avenues of service to us, which are treated more in detail later. The serving Christian is the happy Christian. And as we give our lives in service we receive great blessings in return. "It is more blessed to give than to receive." And here again we have the great Example of our blessed Lord who gave Himself up completely in order that He might be of service to a lost world.

Questions

Why is it necessary that every Christian should be enlisted in active service for the Master?

Name some of the forms of service in which it is the privilege of every Christian to engage.

What are some of the rewards of faithful Christian service?

Chapter Three

CHURCH MEMBERSHIP AND CHRISTIAN ORDINANCES

(It may be well in the case of these longer chapters to divide the material into two, three, or more lessons. The instructor may want to spend considerable time on the ordinances, doctrines, and restrictions. If desired, when the shorter chapters toward the close of the book are reached, two or more may be combined into a single lesson. See pages 10-12 for further instructions as to how to use this book.)

Every one who has accepted Christ as his personal Saviour and Lord will want to take his place with other believers in fellowship and service. God has provided for this in the establishment of the Christian Church. After Jesus ascended to heaven we find that the disciples banded together for fellowship and united worship, and at Pentecost, and afterward, when people repented of their sins and accepted Christ as their Saviour they immediately united with the Church through baptism. We also find that they observed the Christian ordinances. An ordinance has been defined as an outward ceremony with a spiritual meaning. In these things the early Church left an example which every believer should follow.

The visible Church is divided into many different denominations. The believer today has to decide with which particular denomination or church he wants to unite. If he has any difficulty in deciding this it is necessary that he inform himself as to what the different churches believe and teach. It is safe to unite with a church that believes and teaches the whole Bible. The believer will have to decide which church comes nearest to meeting this ideal, according to his understanding of the Scriptures. It is not safe for the convert to delay the matter of selecting and uniting with a church. To delay unnecessarily will be to set himself adrift with nothing to tie to, and the probabilities are that he will soon again be out in the world from which he came. He should attend meetings for the instruction of converts, read his Bible, and pray to God for guidance. Then if he has a willing mind he can rest assured that the Lord will lead him to a church where he can serve his Master acceptably. Unless people unite with a church they will be deprived of the blessings of Christian fellowship with other believers, and of the opportunity of taking part in the ordinances which Christ has commanded His followers to observe.

In the discussions of this chapter we shall consider the following topics: The Church of Christ; Seven Ordinances of the Church—Baptism, Communion, Feet Washing, The Devotional Covering, The Holy Kiss, Anointing with Oil, and Marriage.

I. THE CHURCH OF CHRIST

Outline Study

1. Christ, the Founder of the Church.—Matt. 16:18.
2. The Church, composed of called-out people.—Acts 15:14.
3. A place for fellowship and strengthening of believers.—Acts 2:41-47.
4. The Body of Christ.—Col. 1:18; I Cor. 12:12, 27. See entire chapter.
5. The temple or building of God.—Eph. 2:20-22.
6. The Bride of Christ.—Eph. 5:22-33; Rev. 21:9.
7. The organization and purpose of the Church.— Eph. 4:11-16; Acts 6:1-6; I Tim. 3:1-13; 5:17.
8. The authority of the Church.—Matt. 16:19; 18:18.
   a. To choose its own officials.—Acts 1:15-26; 6: 1-6; 14:23; Tit. 1:5.
   b. To have oversight of its members through its leaders.—Acts 20:28; I Thess. 5:14, 15; Heb. 13:17.
   c. To make decisions and rules for the good of the cause.—Matt. 18:18; Acts 15.
   d. To discipline disobedient members.—Matt. 18: 18; I Cor. 5:1-5; II Thess. 3:6.
9. Jesus' Great Commission to the Church.—Mark 16:15; Matt. 28:19, 20; Acts 1:8.
10. The Church triumphant.—Matt. 16:18.

Practical Comments

The Church of Jesus Christ is the greatest organization existing in the world, because it has Christ as its Founder and Head. Jesus Christ saw that after His departure from the earth His people would need some organization to keep them united in one body, to furnish Christian fellowship and instruction, and to carry on the work of preaching the Gospel to all the people of the world. For this purpose He established His Church, on the foundation of the apostles and prophets, He Himself being the chief Corner Stone. All who hear His voice, come to Him by faith, and follow Him as their Lord, are called out from among the world and their former associations. Then, through public confession of Him as their Saviour, and by baptism as the rite of initiation, all such are received as members of His body, or as parts of His spiritual building. It is a wonderful privilege to be thus closely identified with our Lord Jesus Christ and His people. Through the Church we have fellowship with one another, have the privilege of meeting together for worship and instruction from God's Word, and of working together in the service of our Lord.

The Church is enlarged and strengthened with the addition of every new member. The Christian Church began with a dozen men whom Christ Himself called, but it has grown through the centuries until its members compose a mighty army—a great and powerful organization through which the Lord carries on His work of spreading the Gospel message. The Church is also called the Bride of Christ, thus suggesting that we must be true to Him and watch and wait for His coming, when He will be united with His true followers from whom He is now separated in body but present with His Spirit.

The Church has in its organization various officers or leaders who direct its work. We have in our usual organization bishops, ministers, and deacons. Jesus has given authority to the Church to choose officials from within her ranks, and these are to have the spiritual oversight of the flock. It is their work to care for the members of the Church in seeing that they are instructed in the Word of God, encouraged to press on in the Christian life, and warned against the dangers with which the enemy of souls threatens them. It is also a part of the work of the Church to care for the poor and needy. The members are admonished to submit themselves to those who have the rule over them and to whom they have given the authority of supervision. The Church has authority to make decisions for the strengthening and advancement of the cause, and to discipline disobedient members. The visible Church, as we know it, is composed of imperfect people, but with all that, the Lord has given it authority to carry on His work and has given the promise that all the forces of evil shall never prevail against it. No matter how discouraging things may look at times we may rest assured that the cause of the Lord will triumph at last.

Questions

Who is the Founder of the Christian Church?

Give a definition of the Church.

What is its purpose?

With what authority is the Church vested?

Who gave this authority?

What should be our attitude toward the rules and regulations of the Church?

What is the Great Commission of the Church?

How do we know that the Church will triumph in the end?

II. THE ORDINANCE OF BAPTISM

Outline Study

1. The beginning of baptism in the New Testament. —Matt. 3:1-6; Luke 3:3, 12.
2. Jesus' baptism.—Matt. 3:13-17.
3. Jesus' command to baptize.—Matt. 28:19; Mark 16:15, 16.
4. How the early Church practiced baptism.—Acts 2: 37-41; 8:36-39; 16:33.
5. Water baptism, a type or symbol of the baptism of the Holy Spirit.—Acts 1:5; 2:14-18; 10:44-48; 11:15, 16; I Cor. 12:13.
6. The answer of a good conscience toward God.—I Pet. 3:21.
7. An act of obedience.—Matt. 3:15.
8. Conditions to be met:
   a. Faith.—Acts 8:37.

    b. Repentance.—Acts 2:38.

    c. Conversion.—Acts 9:1-18.

9. Scriptural basis for pouring as the mode of baptism.
—Acts 1:5; 2:1-21; 10:44-48; 11:15, 16; also
compare I Cor. 10:1, 2 and Psa. 77:16-20. The
Spirit was poured out; the water, which is the
symbol, should also be poured out.

Practical Comments

In beginning the study of the ordinances of the
Christian Church we naturally take up baptism first,
because it is the rite or ceremony by which people are
taken into the Church. Baptism as such was not
practiced in Old Testament times, and so we must at
once go to the New Testament Scriptures for the origin, meaning, and practice of this ordinance. The
first mention of water baptism is made concerning
John the Baptist when he began his preaching of repentance in preparing the way for Jesus to begin His
ministry. John baptized great numbers of people who
confessed and repented of their sins, and finally, at
Jesus' urgent request, baptized Him also. Here we
have Jesus' own example, and if it was necessary that
He should be baptized, it should go without saying
that all of us need to be baptized also. He also gave
a positive command to His disciples that they should
baptize all people who believe in Him, in the name
of the Father, the Son, and the Holy Ghost. We find,
then, as we read the history of the early Church in

the book of Acts that the apostles obeyed that command by baptizing many thousands of people who accepted Jesus as their Saviour.

The outward act of baptizing with water stands for certain spiritual things. First of all, it is a type or symbol of the baptism of the believer by the Holy Spirit. This is brought out in the Scriptures a number of times, as the references cited above show. If the baptized person does not have the Holy Spirit in his heart the mere application of the water will be of no value to him. Then again, baptism is "the answer of a good conscience toward God." The person who is baptized thus publicly signifies that he has repented of and confessed his sins, has accepted Christ as his Saviour, has had his sins washed away by the blood of Jesus, and now has a clear conscience, with nothing standing between him and his God. It is also an act of obedience to the commands of the Bible and an evidence that the person wants to follow the example of Jesus. Some of the conditions to be met are, repentance, faith, and conversion, as the foregoing statements show.

An evidence that pouring is the Scriptural mode is found in this that since the Holy Spirit was poured out, the water which stands for the Spirit baptism should likewise be poured. Paul says that the Israelites were baptized when going through the Red Sea; the psalmist in speaking of the same incident says that the "clouds poured out water." The Scriptures, in giving incidents of baptism, say that applicants were baptized with water. This implies that the water was handled rather than the applicant. In none of the incidents of baptism where it is said that the applicants went into the water is it stated that they were under the water. In a number of cases, such as on the day of Pentecost (Acts 2:41), in the house of Cornelius (Acts 10:47, 48), and at the Philippian jail (Acts 16: 33), it is not even intimated that they left the house, much less went to a stream large enough to put some one under the water. We believe the word "pour" gives us the Scriptural idea of the mode of baptism.

Questions

How do we know that baptism is necessary?

Why do we consider it first among the Christian ordinances?

For what spiritual things does the outward act of water baptism stand?

What conditions should the applicant meet before he is qualified to be baptized and received into the Church?

Give reasons for believing that pouring is the Scriptural mode of baptism.

III. THE ORDINANCE OF COMMUNION, OR THE LORD'S SUPPER

Outline Study

1. The communion instituted.—Matt. 26:26-28; Mark 14:22-24; Luke 22:19, 20.

2. What the communion signifies:
   a. A memorial of Christ's broken body and shed blood.—I Cor. 11:23-26.
   b. The unity or oneness of those taking part.—I Cor. 10:16, 17.
   c. A testimony to the Lord's death and coming again.—I Cor. 11:26.
3. A definite command.—Luke 22:19; I Cor. 11:24, 25.
4. A means of strength and blessing to the Christian. —I Cor. 10:16.
5. Conditions to be met by those observing the communion:
   a. Self-examination.—I Cor. 11:28.
   b. Holy life.—I Cor. 10:20, 21; 5:7, 8.
   c. Unity and peace with the brotherhood.—I Cor. 10:17.
6. Results of partaking unworthily.—I Cor. 11:29, 30.

Practical Comments

On the last night before the crucifixion and death of Jesus He and His twelve apostles met in an upper room in Jerusalem to keep the Passover Feast, which was observed once a year in commemoration of the deliverance of the Israelites from the bondage of Egypt. At the close of this feast Jesus instituted a new ordinance which His followers were to observe in commemoration of His suffering and death on the cross to deliver them from the bondage of sin and Satan.

The communion is a memorial service which brings to the remembrance of Christians the sacrifice which Jesus made for them on the cross. It keeps us from forgetting the great work which He did for us when He gave Himself a ransom for our sins. The bread stands for His broken and pierced body, the cup for the blood which He shed for the remission of our sins. Jesus knew that we needed something to keep this great event fresh in our minds. The communion also signifies oneness and unity, which should exist in the Church, the body of Christ. Just as the bread is one mass in which the grains of wheat are united in one common union, so the believers in Christ should be one bread and one body. Every time we observe this ordinance we show to the world that we have accepted the atoning work of Christ on the cross and that we look forward to His coming again to receive His followers to Himself.

Jesus gave definite commands that we should observe the communion, and He gave us this ordinance for a definite purpose. Not only does it bring to our minds the things mentioned above, but it is a means of bringing us new spiritual strength and blessing. It is a cup of blessing, and each time we partake of it we receive new blessings that will help us and strengthen us in our spiritual lives. It is typical of the life which we receive by partaking of the flesh and blood of Christ in a spiritual way. Jno. 6:53-57.

It is a serious thing to partake of the communion, and we are commanded to examine ourselves to see whether we are in proper spiritual condition to take part in it. We should be in right relationship with God and at peace with the brotherhood and man in general as far as is possible. Rom. 12:18. In order to determine the spiritual state of the brotherhood and to see whether the members are in proper condition to observe communion, counsel meetings are held a short time prior to the time of communion.

Since a church can have no jurisdiction over members of other churches we believe it is in harmony with the Scriptures to observe close communion, in which only the members of our own denomination take part. The seriousness of the communion service is further brought out in Biblical statements of the terrible results which follow when people partake of the bread and cup unworthily.

Questions

On what occasion and by whom was the communion instituted?

What are some of the things it stands for?

What things should be done both by individual members and by the Church before the communion is observed?

What are the results when the communion is observed by true believers? By unworthy members?

Why should the Church observe close communion?

IV. THE ORDINANCE OF FEET WASHING

Outline Study

1. The institution of the ordinance of feet washing.—
   Jno. 13:1-17.
2. Meaning of the ordinance:
   a. Humility and Christian equality.—Jno. 13:16.
   b. Mutual service.—Jno. 13:5, 14.
   c. A symbol of the washing from sin by the blood
      of Christ.—Jno. 13:8-10.
3. The direct command.—Jno. 13:14, 15.
4. The promise to those who observe the ordinance.
   —Jno. 13:17.
5. Practiced in apostolic times.—I Tim. 5:10.

Practical Comments

On the same night that Jesus established the communion service He also instituted the ordinance of feet washing. He rose from the table, girded Himself with a towel, poured some water into a basin, and washed the feet of the twelve apostles. They did not understand the meaning of what He did, and when He began, Peter protested very much against Jesus' washing his feet. Jesus told Peter that if he did not allow Him to wash his feet he could have no part with Him. This is also true in the spiritual sense, for if we are not washed from our sins with the blood of Jesus we can never have any part with Him.

Jesus also showed a fine lesson of humility and brotherly equality. At this very supper there had been strife among the disciples as to who should be the greatest among them. He, their Lord and Master, was willing to take the place of a servant among them. They should in like manner serve each other. Instead of striving for the highest place they should humble themselves and be willing to take the lowest place. In washing each other's feet they would show that none esteemed himself above the other, but that all were equal as followers of Jesus and brethren in the Church.

The command that we should observe this ordinance is very plain, and all of us should be willing to follow Jesus' example and wash each other's feet, just as He washed the feet of His disciples. It is very plain that Jesus did not here observe some old custom, otherwise the disciples would have understood what He was about to do. He instituted a new Christian ordinance which He intended His followers to observe, and He has promised happiness and blessing to those who do these things that He has taught.

Questions

On what occasion did Jesus institute the ordinance of feet washing?

What is the ordinance intended to teach or signify?

How do we know that Jesus intended His followers to observe this ordinance?

What is His promise to those who obey the things
    that He says?

How do we know that the apostles practiced this or-
    dinance?

V. THE ORDINANCE OF THE DEVOTIONAL
COVERING

Outline Study

1. The ordinance stated and explained.—I Cor. 11:
    2-16.
2. Its observance requires an artificial covering.—I
    Cor. 11:5, 6, 13.
3. Woman should also preserve the natural covering
    of the hair.—I Cor. 11:14, 15.
4. The purpose of the ordinance.—I Cor. 11:3-5, 10.
5. The apostle's question and conclusion.—I Cor. 11:
    13, 16.
6. The apostle's authority.—I Cor. 14:37.

Practical Comments

We now come to the fourth ordinance in our list
and we find that the Apostle Paul gives us the foundation for this in the first part of I Cor. 11. The ordinance of communion is treated in the latter part of
the chapter. That this is really an ordinance, an outward act or ceremony with a spiritual meaning, is
shown in verse 2. The apostle tells plainly that women

should have their heads covered whenever engaged in prophesying (see I Cor. 14:3 for definition of prophesying) or praying. That this is not the natural covering of the hair is shown very conclusively in I Cor. 11: 6, in which it is stated that if a woman does not have her head covered she might as well also cut off her hair. If the hair were the covering spoken of there would be nothing to shear after she is uncovered. The Revised Version in the use of the word "veiled" also makes this distinction clear. Hair never constitutes a veil. Paul, however, draws a lesson and an illustration from the hair, the natural covering of woman. Long hair is a glory to woman, and it is a shame for her to cut off her hair. Just so in the realm of the spiritual, in the Church of Jesus Christ, it is unbecoming and a dishonor for a woman to pray or prophesy with her head uncovered or unveiled.

By reading the verses carefully we find the purpose of the ordinance, that is, the things which the outward covering or veiling symbolizes. It shows the proper relationship between woman, man, Christ, and God. God is the great Head of all, and the order, going downward, is: God, Christ, man, woman. Man shows his relation to Christ and God by worshiping with his head uncovered. He should not take part in a Christian service with a covering on his head. Woman shows her relation to man, to Christ, and to God by worshiping with her head covered. This is the divine order which every Christian woman should recognize. The covering is a sign of power or authority

(Revised Version), which shows that the woman is taking her rightful place in God's order. The angels take recognition of her submission to the will of God, and she has, acting under the supervision of man, her head and representative before Christ and God in the Church, authority to pray and prophesy. She has both power and authority in her prayer and Christian testimony. Since the covering is a sign it stands for a pure, devoted Christian life and the wearer should by God's grace make her life conform to this standard. Since this is an ordinance of the Church, the Church should decide the form of the covering, since the Scripture gives no exact form. The fact that the covering is a sign also shows that it is a special covering and not a protection covering.

Although the divine order is as outlined above, the apostle on the other hand makes it clear that both man and woman are dependent upon each other, and that both in their proper spheres are responsible to God. He appeals to the judgment of people and asks if it is becoming for a woman to pray to God with unveiled head. And in the concluding verse (I Cor. 11:16) of this discussion, he says that neither he nor the churches of God had any such custom. Some people might be contentious about it, but the authority of the apostle, speaking by inspiration of God, and the practice of the early Christian Church are back of this Christian ordinance.

Questions

How do we know that the devotional covering is one
   of the Christian ordinances?
What outward form is required by this ordinance?
What spiritual things does it stand for?
What other covering is mentioned in this Scripture?
How can you tell that the hair is not the same as the
   devotional covering?
Why does not a protection covering answer the pur-
   pose?

VI. THE ORDINANCE OF THE HOLY KISS

Outline Study

1. The basis for the ordinance.—Rom. 16:16; I Cor.
   16:20; II Cor. 13:12; I Thess. 5:26; I Pet. 5:14.
2. It is a holy greeting.—First four references above.
3. It is a greeting of love.—I Pet. 5:14.
4. It is for all the brethren.—I Thess. 5:26.
5. It was practiced by the early Church.—Acts 20:37.

Practical Comments

Different salutations are mentioned in the Bible.
Some of these refer merely to ordinary greetings among
people as they meet from time to time, and these vary
with the changing customs of people living in different periods of history and in different places. The
greeting of the holy kiss, however, is mentioned spe-

cifically five different times in the New Testament, when it is given in the form of a definite command. We list it among the ordinances, because it is an outward form of greeting which symbolizes the holiness and love that should exist in every Christian heart and serve as a bond of union and fellowship that unites Christian believers. It is just as natural an expression of the fervent love which exists among Christian believers as it is, in a nonreligious sense, a token of the love that exists in family life. It should be observed by "all the brethren." This word is used in a collective way, and sisters should greet sisters in this way as well as the brethren greet brethren. Instances of its use are found in the greeting of Judas to Christ (showing that it must have been the custom among the disciples and Jesus) and Paul and the Ephesian elders. Acts 20:37.

Questions

What Scriptural basis have we for the ordinance of the holy kiss?

How does it differ from ordinary salutations?

Who should observe it?

VII. THE ORDINANCE OF ANOINTING WITH OIL

Outline Study

1. Scriptural foundation for the ordinance.—Jas. 5: 13-16.

2. A suggestion rather than an absolute command.—Verse 14.
3. It is for the healing of the body.—Verses 14, 15.
4. It is to be administered at the request of the afflicted one.—Verse 14.
5. To be administered by the elders of the Church.—Verse 14.
6. It must be coupled with "the prayer of faith."—Verse 15.
7. Hence it is for believing Christians only.—Verses 14, 15.

Practical Comments

This Scripture comes to us more in the form of a suggestion than a direct or absolute command. But it finds a place among the ordinances, since it is an outward religious ceremony which has a spiritual significance. Those who are afflicted in body may, if they are so led, call the leaders of the Church, who are authorized by this Scripture to anoint the sick person with oil, in the name of the Lord. The oil in itself is not intended to work a cure, but simply to serve as a symbol of the healing power of God. This ordinance is not intended as something that should be observed just before death by people who have no hopes of getting well, but is coupled with the "prayer of faith" in such a way that we believe no one should call for its administration unless he has faith that the Lord will heal him. This same principle of prayer and faith also implies that only a believing person, a true

Christian, is eligible to be anointed with oil for the healing of the body. This excludes infants and people who have never accepted Christ as their Saviour. Since the thought of confession of sins is also given in verse 16 we get the idea that the one who calls for the anointing should confess all his sins and be sure that he is in close fellowship with God. The persons who perform the ceremony, as well as all those in attendance, should also have faith that God will hear their prayers and heal the afflicted one. However, in observance of this ordinance as well as in all other things we should have the attitude of our Saviour and of the early Church: "The will of the Lord be done." As people grow in the Christian life and come into closer fellowship with God they will no doubt find more and more occasion to carry out this divine suggestion for the healing of the sick.

Questions

Why should anointing with oil be listed among the ordinances?

What is the purpose of the ordinance?

For whom is it intended?

Who alone are authorized to administer it?

What conditions must be present if it is to accomplish its purpose?

VIII. THE ORDINANCE OF MARRIAGE

Outline Study

1. Origin of marriage.—Gen. 2:20-24; Mark 10:6-9.
2. Its purpose.—Gen. 1:27, 28; 2:18.
3. Marriage between near relatives forbidden.—Lev. 18:1-18.
4. Marriage between believers and unbelievers forbidden.—Deut. 7:1-4; Josh. 23:11-13; Ezra 10:10-12; Neh. 13:23-26; I Cor. 7:39; II Cor. 6:14.
5. Marriage is a sacred bond between one man and one woman, lasting until one or the other dies. —Mark 10:6-9; I Cor. 7:39.
6. New Testament teaching against divorce and remarriage.—Matt. 19:7-9; Mark 10:2-12; Luke 16:18; Rom. 7:2, 3; I Cor. 7:39.
7. Polygamy has no place in New Testament teaching. —I Cor. 7:2.

Practical Comments

Marriage is the earliest institution which God gave for the benefit of man. It is classed among the ordinances because it carries with it an outward ceremony which binds two lives together as long as both live. God saw that it was not good for the man to be alone, and so He made mankind male and female in order that they might be of help to each other and continue the human race. Marriage is not compulsory, but is given for the help and blessing of all who enter into this God-ordained relationship. God in His Word has also given certain rules and restrictions concerning marriage. Marriage between near relatives is forbidden. So also is marriage between believers and unbelievers. All through the history of God's people we notice that when this rule was violated the result was spiritual loss and in many cases disaster. The Old Testament references abundantly confirm this. In the New Testament believers are plainly told to marry "only in the Lord," and are warned against being "unequally yoked together with unbelievers." Reasons for this are: The unbelieving partner in marriage has a continual tendency to lead the believing one away from the faith, and the home is not in position to bring up children in the "nurture and admonition of the Lord" as the Scriptures command.

Marriage is a sacred bond that God intends shall endure as long as both of the contracting parties live. The Scripture teachings against divorce and remarriage are very plain and emphatic, although separation is allowed if one or the other person is unfaithful to the marriage vow. However, in no Scripture is remarriage of separated or divorced persons tolerated, unless they reunite with their former companions. The teaching is that if a divorced person remarries while his former companion is living he is guilty of adultery. The proper thing for a divorced person to do is to become reconciled to the original companion. I Cor. 7:10, 11. Polygamy, having more than one wife, was allowed in the Old Testament, but the New Testament gives no sanction to this practice, which led to much sorrow and unhappiness in Old Testament times. Marriage is a Christian institution, and it is important that every one should be informed as to the Scriptural teaching concerning it. In this way much unhappiness and many a spiritual disaster may be averted.

Questions

When was marriage instituted?

What is its purpose?

Why should there be no marriage of believers with unbelievers?

How long should the marriage bond last?

What is the Scriptural teaching about divorce, remarriage, and polygamy?

Chapter Four

CHRISTIAN PRINCIPLES AND RESTRICTIONS

We assume that the applicant has begun the Christian life in all sincerity, that he accepts the ordinances of the Christian Church, and that it is his desire to observe them as the opportunity presents itself. There are yet many other things that he should know, and in this chapter we aim to give some of the most important Christian principles and restrictions. In the Christian life, as in other matters, we find both the positive and the negative principles and commands. Thus we find some principles that require positive action and others that are expressed in restrictions. However, even these restrictions also have a positive side which requires action to make them effective. Nonresistance is merely love in action. Nonconformity to the world requires positive conformity to the standards of the Gospel of Jesus Christ. Included in this chapter will be found a group of important doctrines of the Church, some of which are rather unpopular, but which are nevertheless based upon the Word of God. The Christian Principles and Restrictions which we shall here discuss are: Obedience, Worship, Nonresistance to Evil, Nonconformity to the World, Nonswearing of Oaths, Nonsecrecy, Nonparticipation in Life Insurance.

I. OBEDIENCE

Outline Study

1. Obedience to God.—I Sam. 15:22; Matt. 7:21; Acts 5:29; Jno. 14:23.
2. Obedience to the Church.—Heb. 13:17; Matt. 18:17.
3. Obedience to parents.—Eph. 6:1.
4. Obedience to other authorities.—Col. 3:22; Tit. 3: 1; Rom. 13:1.
5. The true motive of obedience.—Jno. 14:15; 15:14.
6. Blessings of obedience to God.—Matt. 12:50; Jno. 7:17; 14:23; Acts 5:32; Jas. 1:25; Rev. 22:14.
7. Results of disobedience.—Eph. 5:6; II Thess. 1:8; Heb. 2:2, 3.

Practical Comments

Having decided to live for God, through acceptance of Christ as our Saviour and Lord, a life of obedience naturally follows. Just as before conversion a person naturally follows the dictates of the world, the flesh, and the devil, so after conversion as he acknowledges the right of the Father, the Son, and the Holy Spirit to rule and direct his life, it will be his desire to live in obedience to the Trinity of God. The commands of the Bible concerning Christian obedience are very plain, and God not only requires but delights in the obedience of His people. Our supreme allegiance belongs to God, our Creator, who redeemed us through His Son, and gives us the Holy Spirit to teach and to guide us. We certainly owe Him our whole-hearted obedience, both as a duty and a privilege, for He requires nothing of us but what is the very best for us.

The Bible also teaches obedience to the Church of Christ, the body which He established upon earth to carry on His work. Christ has delegated certain power and authority to the Church, and He recognizes in heaven the actions which the Church takes on earth. Matt. 16:19; 18:18. We are also told to be obedient to our parents, to our masters for whom we work, and to the authorities of the temporal government. This is all according to the will of God, and when we render obedience to the constituted authorities we are really rendering obedience to God.

The true motive of obedience is not force or outside pressure but love within the heart for the person to whom obedience is rendered. The proper child will obey its parents because it loves them. We will obey the laws of the land because of our love for the right. Similarly, if we love God and Christ we will obey the commandments of God's Word. This is the test which Jesus gave by which we may know if we love Him. If we fail to obey His commandments it is idle to say that we love Him, for such professions of love are not from the heart.

God's Word promises great blessings to those who obey Him. Some of these are: admission to the family of God; a knowledge of His will; the love and presence of the Father and Son; the gift of the Holy Spirit; the blessings of God on our work; and admission into the Holy City in the eternal world. On the other hand, disobedience brings upon us the wrath of God and eventually the flaming fire of His vengeance.

Questions

To whom should we render obedience?

Why is obedience an important Christian principle?

What is the true motive of obedience?

What are some of the blessings?

What is the result of disobedience to God?

Give some examples of both obedience and disobedience.

II. WORSHIP

Outline Study

1. What worship is.—Ex. 4:31; II Chron. 7:3; Neh. 8:6.
2. The command to worship God.—Matt. 4:10; Heb. 1:6.
3. The worship of idols forbidden. Ex. 20:4; Deut. 11:16.
4. God seeks true worshipers.—Jno. 4:23.
5. How to worship.—Psa. 29:2; Jno. 4:24; Phil. 3:3.
6. Where to worship.—Jno. 4:20-24; Heb. 10:25; Psa. 99:9.
7. Results of true worship:
   a. Spiritual satisfaction and joy.—Psa. 27:4.

b. Partaking of the likeness and glory of God.—
   II Cor. 3:18.
c. Strength.—Isa. 40:31
d. Christian fellowship.—Acts 2:42-47.

Practical Comments

True worship is an attitude of heart in which the soul bows before God in adoration and reverence. If the worship is false something other than God is the object adored. Singing, praying, preaching, reading the Bible, meditation, are all activities that should lead us to worship, although in themselves they may not be worship. In worship we are occupied with the glory, majesty, greatness, and goodness of God Himself. God alone is a proper object of worship. This includes the Son and the Holy Spirit, for they also are God. The worship of idols is absolutely forbidden in God's Word, because such worship leads people away from God and to spiritual ruin. Anything upon which we set our affections to such an extent as to crowd out God becomes idolatry. Some things of this type in modern times are: wealth, pleasure, fame, lust, self. But God is seeking true worshipers, and the soul that responds to His call and command to worship is not only performing one of the highest duties given to man but is enjoying one of the greatest of all human blessings. Let us remember that worship is a definite command of God.

Worship, in order to be pleasing and acceptable to God, must be sincere and true, and such worship can only be performed by the help of the Spirit of God. We must realize our own helplessness properly to see God in His greatness and glory, and we should ask Him to reveal Himself to us by His Spirit and lead us into praise and adoration and worship. We can worship God anywhere—in the home, in the office, on the farm, or in public assemblies. We should have our private worship, but we dare not neglect regular attendance upon public worship in the house of the Lord, for it is there that we worship Him in a way such as we can not enjoy at any other time or place.

The heart that truly responds to God's call to worship finds a spiritual joy and satisfaction that can be found in no other way. As we think and meditate upon the glory of God, we are transformed more and more into His likeness and thus have a share in His glory. Through worship we receive strength for the cares, trials, and duties of life, and in public worship we not only enjoy the fellowship of God but a blessed Christian fellowship with each other. True worship is the secret of spiritual power.

Questions

What is worship?

Whom should we worship?

What is idolatry?

What constitutes true worship?

What is the proper time and place to worship?
Name some of the results of true worship.

III. NONRESISTANCE TO EVIL

Outline Study

1. Prophecies concerning Christ's peaceable reign.—
   Isa. 2:4; 9:6, 7; 52:7.
2. Jesus' own teaching.—Matt. 5:38-48; 26:51, 52;
   Luke 9:56; Jno. 18:36.
3. Teaching of the apostles.—Rom. 12:17-21; II Cor.
   10:3, 4, I Pet. 2:19-24; 3:8, 9.
4. The end of the law.—Luke 16:16; Jno. 1:17; Rom.
   10:4.
5. Examples of Christ and the early Church.—Matt.
   26:52, 53; I Pet. 2:21-24; Acts 7:54-60.
6. The positive side.—Matt. 5:44; 22:39, 40; Rom.
   12:20, 21; 13:7-10; Eph. 6:10-18.

Practical Comments

Centuries before Jesus came to earth as a little
child, the prophets foretold of His coming as the
Prince of Peace, of the Gospel of peace which He
should bring, and of the peaceable nature of His kingdom. And when He began to teach and to preach we
find that what He said was in harmony with these
prophecies. He taught very plainly that His followers
should not resist evil, should not sue at law, and should

go the second mile in doing more than people ask of them. His teaching against war is very positive. He commanded Peter to put up his sword and said that all who fight with the sword should perish in the same way. He made it clear that He came to save men's lives, not to destroy them, and that His kingdom was not of this world. For that reason His servants should not fight.

The apostles in their later writings taught the same principles regarding resistance to evil treatment by others. Paul says very plainly that we should not render evil for evil to any man, and that we should have no part in the use of carnal weapons. Peter cities the example of Christ who took patiently all the evil treatment that His enemies heaped upon Him, even dying upon the cross for their sakes. No matter how they reviled Him, He gave back no angry word, but prayed for them instead.

Why did Jesus teach a principle which was not taught in the Old Testament? Because He was the Son of God and had authority to give the laws for the governing of His kingdom which He came to set up. The law of Moses was in force until He came and gave the law of nonresistance to evil. Christ is the end of the law to every one who believes, and now we follow Him and His teachings. However, many of the laws of the Old Testament have been carried over into and are sanctioned by the New Testament, which is our guide of life in this dispensation.

We not only have the example of Jesus in carrying out this principle which He taught, but the example of the apostles and other early Church leaders as well. Stephen, when he was ill-treated and stoned, prayed, like the Saviour, that the Lord would not lay this sin to the charge of his persecutors. The apostle Paul in all his experiences of ill-treatment did not return evil for evil. In the teaching of the New Testament, both in precept and practice, we find the doctrine of nonresistance an outstanding one.

The positive side of this teaching is that when people mistreat us, we should, in spite of their evil deeds, love them, pray for them, and do good to them. The Christian, like his Master, should spend his time in doing good to others, and, having that spirit of love in his heart, he will not retaliate when evil treatment and persecution come his way. He has no use for carnal weapons, but has the Christian armor of Eph. 6:10-18. Using that he will trust the Lord to care for him every time he meets with evil treatment. Psa. 91.

Questions

What are the New Testament teachings concerning personal fighting, going to law, and war?

Do these differ in some things from the teachings of Old Testament times?

Who changed them? Why?

What can you say about the positive side of nonresistance?

IV. NONCONFORMITY TO THE WORLD

Outline Study

1. The god of this world.—Jno. 12:31; II Cor. 4:4.
2. Worldly characteristics.—Eph. 2:2, 3; I Pet. 4:3; I Jno. 2:16, 17.
3. The believer's position.—Jno. 17:14-16.
4. Not to have fellowship with or to love the world.— Matt. 6:24; Jas. 4:4; I Jno. 2:15.
5. To be separate from the world.—II Cor. 6:14-18; Jas. 1:27.
6. Not to be conformed to the world.—Rom. 12:2.
7. To abstain from worldly clothing and jewelry.— I Tim. 2:9, 10; I Pet. 3:3, 4.
8. The transformed life through the renewed mind.— Rom. 12:2; Eph. 4:22-24.
9. The life yielded to God overcomes the world.— Rom. 6:11-13; I Jno. 5:4, 5.

Practical Comments

The term "world" as used in this discussion refers to the things of this life that are evil. There are two kingdoms—the kingdom of God and the kingdom of this world—and all of us belong to one or the other. Satan is the god or prince of this world. His works are altogether evil and are designed for the destruction of the souls of men. His kingdom is characterized by every evil work that one can imagine.

Scripture sometimes gives lists of these things. Some of them are: unbelief, disobedience, pride, lying, profanity, evil speaking, stealing, murder, immorality, covetousness, fashionable attire and jewelry, sinful amusements, fighting, etc. The believer in Christ is not of this world and should keep from all its evils. He should have no fellowship with it, nor love it. To do so is to be an enemy of God. We cannot serve two masters at once. And if we love the world we will serve it and hate our Lord Jesus Christ.

God saw that the world is the greatest enemy of His people and that unless they are on their guard they will be overcome by its evil influences. Hence He gave warnings in His Word that we do well to heed. He has told His followers to keep separate from worldly entanglements and to keep unspotted from the evils that are about us. To be yoked together with worldly people in business, politics, close friendships, associations, marriage, or in other ways will be sure to lead us into worldly things—dishonesty, amusements, pride, etc.—that will do us great spiritual harm and possibly cause our spiritual ruin.

And so we should live separate from the world and not be conformed to it in any way. To conform means to follow the forms or fashions of the world and to be in harmony and agreement with the standards of the world. To refuse to do this is called nonconformity.

Conformity to the world includes many things, quite a number of which have already been referred to. The world has many forms and fashions, but we want to call especial attention to the matter of dress. The Revised Version of Rom. 12:2 makes the application to dress plainer than the Authorized Version, in this language: "And be not fashioned according to this world." Other Scriptures condemn pride and immodesty in clothing, and the Christian should fashion his clothes according to the Bible standards of modesty, decency, usefulness, and simplicity. This excludes clothing that displays parts of the body and that is made for pride and show rather than for simplicity and service. Since the world dictates the fashions of clothing that worldly people wear, the Church certainly has a right to prescribe what sort of clothing best conforms to the Bible standards. For this reason the Church has prescribed some forms of clothing, and applicants are expected to conform to the standards of dress as found in our conference rules. These standards of dress are in harmony with Scriptural principles. Concerning the wearing of jewelry such Scriptures as Isa. 3:18-23; I Tim. 2:9; I Pet. 3:3 give the basis for the rule of the Church against this practice. Fashionable and fantastic wearing of the hair is also ruled against on similar Scriptural grounds, it being specifically mentioned in some of these Scripture passages. ·

The positive side of the life that is not conformed to this world comes through being conformed to the things of God. This is brought about by being transformed by the renewing of the mind through the new life in Christ Jesus. If we yield ourselves in full submission to God, making no provision to fulfill the lusts of the flesh, and live a life of faith in Jesus as our Saviour, Lord, and Advocate, we will overcome the world. "This is the victory that overcometh the world, even our faith" (I Jno. 5:4).

Questions

What is the meaning of "nonconformity to the world"?

Why should we not be conformed to the world?

What are some of the principal characteristics of the world?

What evils result when Christians assume friendly relations with the world?

What is the correct Christian attitude toward the world in the sense that we use it here?

What is the Christian principle concerning the fashions of the world?

What is the Bible teaching about jewelry?

What is the secret of victory over the world?

V. NONSWEARING OF OATHS

Outline Study

1. Profanity always forbidden.—Ex. 20:7.
2. Jesus' teaching concerning all kinds of oaths. Matt. 5:33-37.
3. Apostolic teaching.—Tit. 3:8; Jas. 5:12.
4. Our attitude.—Jno. 14:15; Acts 5:29.

Practical Comments

God in the third one of the Ten Commandments says that no one shall take the name of the Lord in vain, for He will hold every one guilty who does so. It is a gross sin to use the name of the Lord irreverently or to speak of sacred things in a blasphemous, frivolous, or light manner. However, in Old Testament times it was permissible to use the judicial or legal oath, in which a person would solemnly swear by the name of the Lord that what he said or was about to say was true. Num. 30:2; Deut. 6:13. But when Jesus gave the laws of His kingdom in the Sermon on the Mount He forbade His followers to use any kind of oath. His command is, "Swear not at all." This includes the profane oath, the judicial oath, and the so-called "wooden oath," or byword in which the person speaking uses other names than that of the Deity. Our speech should be a simple statement of fact, "yes" and "no," for what is more than that comes of evil. The apostle James says practically the same thing, also making it emphatic that we should not swear in any way, lest we "fall into condemnation."

The laws of the land do not require any one to take the legal oath. Any one who does not wish to lift up his hand and swear to tell the truth, as he is about to give testimony or to sign a legal document, may affirm, which is merely a matter of saying "yes" to the question as to whether he will tell the truth. Paul in writing to Titus speaks of affirming. The difference between the affirmation and the legal oath, as far as Christians are concerned, is that the one is according to the teachings of Christ and the other is not.

Why did Jesus make this change in rules for the conduct of God's people? It may be because the Gospel standards are so much higher than those of Old Testament times that no Christian should need to take an oath to guarantee that he is telling the truth. He should tell the truth at all times, and thus make the oath absolutely unnecessary. But whether we know the reason or not, we may be assured that it was for the best interests of His people, and we should gladly obey His Word whether we understand it or not. "But above all things, my brethren, swear not" (Jas. 5:12).

Questions

Name two different kinds of oaths.
Which one was permitted in Old Testament times?
Are oaths allowed in the Gospel dispensation?
What should be our attitude on this question?

VI. NONSECRECY

Outline Study

1. Secrecy is wrong in principle.—Matt. 5:15, 16; Luke 8:17; 11:33; Jno. 3:19; 18:20.
2. The lodge requires the oath, which is unscriptural. —Lev. 5:4, 5; Matt. 5:33-37; Jas. 5:12.

3. The lodge shows respect of persons.—Jno. 6:37; Matt. 11:28; Jas. 2:9; Gal. 6:10.
4. The evil of the unequal yoke.—II Cor. 6:14, 15; Eph. 5:11, 12; Jas. 4:4; I Pet. 4:3-5.
5. The fallacy of hopes of salvation apart from Christ. —Jno. 3:5; 14:6; Acts 4:12.
6. Divided allegiance and time which belong to the home and Church.—Eph. 5:25, 28; I Tim. 5:8; Matt. 6:24; 23:8.
7. The whole system of secret societies is built on the wrong foundation.—Matt. 16:18; I Cor. 3:11.
8. Secretism bears the wrong kind of fruit.—Matt. 7: 16-20; 15:13.

Practical Comments

The whole system of secret societies or lodges is based on the wrong principle. Good people and good organizations do not need to conceal their deeds. Jesus said that we should not hide our light under a bushel but should put it to a place where it can be of use. If we are to be a light unto the world as He was and as He commanded us to be, we cannot hide inside the walls of a secret lodge, doing things that we want no one to know. Jesus taught openly and had nothing to say or to do that was to be kept secret. His acts and words are to be published to all people. He condemned secrecy on the ground that people who practiced it did so because they were guilty of evil deeds.

One of the first reasons that a Christian can have no part in secret societies is because these societies require the use of the oath, which the New Testament strictly forbids. The nature of the lodge is such, since the person must swear to forever keep secret things which have not yet been revealed to him, that it is even forbidden in the Old Testament. Lev. 5:4, 5. Then again the lodge shows respect of persons. Lodges make great claims to charitable deeds of many kinds, but only people who pass a successful physical examination are allowed to become members. In some lodges certain races are debarred, thus fostering race prejudice. The Gospel invitation goes out to all men of all races and classes and shows no respect of persons. The Christian standard is to do good to all men, not certain classes or races.

Then again in quite a number of lodges we find many classes of people mingled together—Jew, Gentiles, Christians, heathen religionists, infidels, etc. Christians belonging to such lodges are violating the principle of the unequal yoke. The Bible teaching is that we should keep separate from such organizations, and have no fellowship with them, but rather reprove them. Lodges often hold out false hopes of salvation to their members. People are led to think that their lodge membership will suffice to take them to heaven. When members die, no matter how sinful they may have been, they are committed to the "grand lodge above" and people think they can be saved apart from Jesus Christ and His Church.

The lodge divides the time and allegiance which the Christian owes to his home and his church. In proportion as the church member attends to his lodge meetings and affairs he is robbing either his home or his church of time, devotion, and money. "No man can serve two masters," said Jesus, and a man can not be a good lodge member and at the same time do for his home and church what he ought to do.

The secret lodge is built on the wrong foundation. Some lodges do not allow the name of Christ to be used in their meetings for fear of offending some of their members who do not believe in Christ. Christ is the true foundation, and the Church is built upon Him as the Rock which will forever stand. We have no need of secret organizations to care for the needy or to provide a place where we meet as brothers. Let us build on the sure foundation and have nothing to do with worldly organizations who ignore our Saviour and Lord and His plain teachings. We may know by the fruits of the lodge system—broken or neglected homes, cold church members, false hopes and teachings, secret thwartings of justice, secret empires that work against the government, and many other evils— that they are not of God. Let us honor Him and keep separate from ungodly institutions.

We realize that not all lodges are alike. Some are extremely corrupt and vicious; others seem quite respectable, but all come under the condemnation of Scripture under one or more of the heads outlined above. Labor unions, farmers' organizations, and other nonsecret or semisecret organizations also often have some of these characteristics and should be avoided by Christian people.

Questions

What is wrong with the principles of the secret society system?

Name some of the points in which secret lodges are unscriptural.

What are some evil fruits that the system bears?

VII. NONPARTICIPATION IN LIFE INSURANCE

Outline Study

1. God's methods for caring for His people:
   a. Individual industry and thrift.—Eph. 4:28; I Thess. 4:11, 12; II Thess. 3:10-12.
   b. Near relatives.—I Tim. 5:4, 8.
   c. The Church.—Rom. 12:13; Gal. 6:2, 10.
   d. His own sure promises to the needy.—Jer. 49: 11; Psa. 37:35; Matt. 6:24-34; Phil. 4:19; Heb. 13:5.
2. Where life insurance falls short of the Gospel standard:
   a. It appeals to the covetous nature of man.— Mark 7:21-23; Eph. 5:3; II Pet. 2:3.
   b. It has in it an element of chance or gambling. —Gen. 3:19; Rom. 12:17b.

    c. Its claims to true charity are false.—I Cor. 13:8.

    d. It is contrary to the principle of Christian stewardship.—Hag. 2:8; Matt. 26:19; Luke 16:2.

    e. It undermines trust in God.—Psa. 118:8; Jer. 17:5; I Pet. 5:7.

Practical Comments

Some of the more conservative churches have for many years held that nonparticipation in the life insurance system is a Christian principle that should be observed. We give some of the reasons for this in the outline above and in these comments. In the first place we find that God has made ample provision to care for the earthly needs of His people through the methods which He gives in His Word, and that there is therefore no need of resorting to worldly institutions. Bible teaching makes it plain that it is the duty of every one to work, earn, and save so that he may have sufficient means to take care of his own temporal needs and to give to those who are in need. Near relatives are also given the charge to care for the needy in their families as far as they can. And then the Church has a special obligation to take care of those in need "who are of the household of faith." Back of these and other methods which the Lord may call into play to care for those who put their trust in Him, we have His sure promises that He will care for the widow and the fatherless, will add all the things that we need unto us if we seek first the kingdom of God, and that He will never leave nor forsake us.

Life insurance is a system that the world has called into being for the care of the needy ones, especially widows, orphans, or others who might be left in hard circumstances through the death of some one who was a means of support. It is a worldly organization and may be the best that the world has to offer along this line, but it falls short of the Gospel standard on quite a number of points. Hence, the right and proper thing for Christians to do is not to be yoked up with worldly organizations of this type but to trust the Lord for their care in all circumstances in life. Life insurance appeals to the desire of people to get money without making a reasonable outlay of capital or labor, and back of it is the scheme of its promoters to acquire wealth at the expense of the masses of people, as is evidenced by the high salaries paid to officials and the immense buildings and other expensive equipment which life insurance companies have. The element of chance enters in, for in the case of an early death people may receive a large amount of money when but a small amount was paid in. This has in it the nature of gambling upon life and death, while God's Word tells us we should acquire our living and possessions by honest toil, giving adequate returns for what we receive. Gifts and inheritance are other means of acquiring possessions which are approved by the Bible. Life insurance is not a system which in charity helps the needy, for often at times when it is most needed, through lapsed policies it fails the person who paid in his hard-earned money. "Charity never faileth." Life insurance has been proved a poor investment by those who have carefully investigated the whole system. (See "Life Insurance," by Herbert N. Troyer, Mennonite Publishing House, Scottdale, Pa., price 35 cents.) Christian stewardship requires that the best use be made of the means that God blesses us with, and hence we should keep clear of a wasteful system like life insurance, which makes most of its money from the poorer classes who can least afford to give it.

As a whole it undermines trust in God, because instead of looking to Him for help and support in the time of need, we look to a man-made institution that does not meet the high standards of Christian living as they are set forth in the Bible. "It is better to trust in the Lord than to put confidence in man." May we let nothing undermine our implicit trust in the God who created us, redeemed us, and promised to care for us.

Questions

What provisions has God made for the care of His people?

What are some of the promises which He has given?

Does life insurance meet the standards of God's Word?

In what ways does it fall short?

In what cardinal principle is it especially weakening to the Christian?

Chapter Five

CHRISTIAN LIFE AND CONDUCT

Things to Do and to Avoid

Having learned some of the Christian principles and restrictions that are given in God's Word for the guidance and help of the Christian, the young convert will now be directed to other matters which relate to the proper conduct of the Christian. All people, even the unconverted, usually have some definite ideas as to the right and proper conduct of Christians. But these ideas may not always be in harmony with the teachings of the Bible. It is important, then, that the person starting out in the Christian life should have a few plain Christian teachings concerning Christian conduct. In the matter of conduct or behavior there are certain things that should be done in order to meet the standards of God's Word. On the other hand, there are also a number of things that must be avoided if one is to succeed in the Christian life. In this chapter we shall discuss both the positive and the negative aspects of the subject. We want to consider the following subjects under the general heading of this chapter: The Pure Life; Lights to the World; Temptation; Amusements; Persecution; Guidance; Proper Vocations in Life; The Victorious Life.

I. THE PURE LIFE

Keep thyself pure.—I Tim. 5:22.

The teaching of the Bible is very emphatic that the Christian should lead a pure life. It is very important that we should know just what constitutes a pure life; otherwise we will be in ignorance as to how to live it. To live a pure life, of course, we must have pure hearts. Jesus Himself said, "Blessed are the pure in heart: for they shall see God." Having our hearts cleansed by the blood of Jesus, we must keep them pure if we would lead pure lives. Hence we must keep our affections and thoughts pure. With these very fountains of life kept pure we will have little trouble with the outward manifestations of impurity. However, we should watch our speech so that nothing vulgar, profane, bitter, slanderous, untruthful, or unbecoming escapes from our lips. We should associate with pure-minded people and keep our social relations pure. In this connection it should be stated that vile literature, indecent pictures, movies, theaters, etc., should find no place in the life of the Christian. Undue familiarity between the sexes should be avoided and all places, such as the movie and swimming pool, where indecent exposures of the body are in evidence. Avoid places of temptation and above all else, "Keep thyself pure."

II. LIGHTS TO THE WORLD

Ye are the light of the world.—Matt. 5:14.

Jesus Himself is the Light of the world. In Him alone dwell light and life and truth in their fullness. But it is also His plan and desire that His followers should be lights to the world. One of His direct commands is, "Let your light so shine before men, that they may see your good works, and glorify your Father which is in heaven" (Matt. 5:16). The thought is that we should live according to the teaching and example of Christ in such a way that His influence is extended by our lives. If we profess to be Christians but live just as we did before, so that people can tell no difference in our life and conduct from that of people of the world, we certainly are not a light to the world. But if people see the light and truth of Christ reflected in our lives they will see the beauty and happiness and joy and purity of the Christian life and will be drawn toward the better life. They will see our good works and glorify Jesus and the Father in heaven. The world is reading our lives rather than the Bible, and unless our lives reflect the light of Jesus we will by our walk and conduct and influence lead people the wrong way instead of leading them to Jesus, the Saviour and light of the world. He is the only One who can lead them from the darkness of sin to the light of life. Let your light shine for Jesus in all that you do wherever you may be.

III. TEMPTATION

Watch ye and pray, lest ye enter into temptation.—Mark 14:38.

Temptation comes to every life. Jesus Himself went through some of the fiercest temptations that one could think of, but He overcame the tempter at every point. He knows just what it is to be tempted and can sympathize with us and help us in our temptations. We have two great conflicting forces in the world—the forces of right, with God as the Head, and the forces of evil, with Satan as the leader. Life is a conflict. We find temptations, dangers, and snares everywhere. These are the means which Satan uses to try to cause us to sin, to destroy our usefulness, or to cause us to wreck our spiritual lives altogether.

But it is no sin to be tempted. The old saying is that we cannot keep the birds from flying over our heads, but we can keep them from building nests there. The best things in life come through struggle and battle. And so even in temptations great blessings come to us if we overcome. The oak that stands the severest storm has the strongest wood. We become stronger in our faith and life as we overcome in the struggles against the evil one and the temptations which he puts into our path. But we should never willfully go into the way of temptation and expect God to take care of us. However, when temptations come to us as we go about our duties in life God will take care of us, for He has said that with every temptation He will make a way of escape. I Cor. 10: 13. Let us look to Jesus who is able to help us in every time of need, and we may rest assured that by His help we may conquer every foe. Let us bravely fight the battle against sin and wrong, knowing that each victory will make us stronger and bring blessings into our lives. "Yield not to temptation."

IV. AMUSEMENTS

Whether therefore ye eat, or drink, or whatsoever ye do, do all to the glory of God.—I Cor. 10:31.

This is an age of the world in which we have many forms of amusement. The Christian, and especially the young Christian, must be on the watch with regard to these. Theaters, movies, dances, card games, pool rooms, various kinds of questionable entertainments, swimming pools where sexes intermingle in the scantiest attire, and other worldly amusements are continually making their bid for our young people to patronize them. There are recreational activities and gatherings that are wholesome and helpful. Patronize these and avoid the harmful ones. Here are a number of rules given by R. A. Torrey which we do well to apply to the amusement question:

1. "Do not indulge in any form of amusement about whose propriety you have any doubts." If you are not sure that it is right and good leave it alone.

2. "Do not engage in any amusement that you cannot engage in to the glory of God." This is a fine

test to put to the matter of going to any form of entertainment or gathering.

3. "Do not engage in any amusement that will hurt your influence with anybody." Even if it might not hurt you, think of what effect it might have upon some weaker person.

4. "Do not engage in any amusement that you cannot make a matter of prayer."

5. "Do not go to any place of amusement where you cannot take Christ with you, and where you do not think Christ would feel at home."

6. "Do not engage in any amusement that you would not like to be found enjoying if the Lord should come."

7. "Do not engage in any amusement, no matter how harmless it would be for yourself, that might harm some one else."

We believe these simple rules will guide you right in the matter of amusements, conversation, and daily life and work.

V. PERSECUTION

Blessed are they which are persecuted for righteousness' sake.—Matt. 5:10.

Every true Christian will some time or other have to suffer persecution, that is, suffer in some way because of his loyalty to Christ. In the times of the apostles people were imprisoned, beaten, exiled, and sometimes killed because of their faith. The same conditions prevailed in the time of the Reformation when Menno Simons and other leaders took a stand for Christ. In our day persecution has subtler forms, although at times, as in the World War, violent persecution also breaks out. More often it is in the form of ridicule, opposition on the part of members of the family or friends, and being dropped from certain social circles. Sometimes it may mean the giving up of some kinds of work, because employers often discharge people who refuse to work on the Lord's Day or otherwise take a positive stand on Bible principles.

However, persecution, no matter how severe, should not discourage the young Christian. Rather, he should rejoice that he is counted worthy to suffer for his Master's sake. Jesus was persecuted, the apostles were persecuted, the faithful of all ages have had to suffer persecution. We should rejoice that we are privileged to follow in their steps. "All that will live godly in Christ Jesus shall suffer persecution" (II Tim. 3:12).

VI. GUIDANCE

He will guide you into all truth.—Jno. 16:13.

The first essential in guidance is that the Christian should be fully surrendered or yielded to the will of God. There must be a desire to know the will of God and a willingness to follow Him wherever He may lead. The question now comes, "How may we know what the will of God is for our lives?" The answer includes a number of points.

1. Prayer. God has promised if we lack wisdom He will give us liberally if we ask. Jas. 1:5-7. We should recognize our own inability to guide our lives aright without the help of God, and then come to Him in faith and ask Him to guide us.

2. The Holy Spirit. God gives the Holy Spirit to us to guide us into all truth. Let us fullfill the conditions for receiving the Spirit and then follow His leading at all times.

3. Consultation with Christian people, especially those of more experience. In this list should be included parents, teachers, ministers, and other godly friends. If God reveals the same things to other people that we believe He has revealed to us, we have a confirmation of His leading. He often guides us through the counsel of godly people.

4. The Church. The Church may call us to special work. We can take this as God's definite leading for our lives.

5. The Word. The Word is given as a lamp to our feet and a light to our path. Psa. 119:105. Here God gives us principles that will apply to every circumstance in life. Let us be sure to test every leading by the Word. If it fails here we may know it is not of God. If it is in harmony with the Word and the other means of guidance enumerated here, we may rest in faith that it is the will of God.

VII. PROPER VOCATIONS IN LIFE

If any would not work, neither should he eat.—II Thess. 3:10.

God's Word teaches that every one should be engaged in earning a livelihood; that is, he should give some service in some way to others in return for which he receives money or other materials by which his daily needs are supplied. For young people especially it is important to know that the Bible teaches industry, economy, and thrift, and that it condemns very severely laziness and depending upon others for a living.

We should look to the Lord to guide us into a life vocation that is in accordance with His will and in which we can serve Him best. Some occupations or kinds of business have unscriptural features about them (such as working on the Lord's Day, catering to worldly and sinful tendencies in man, and serving no useful purpose in the world) that should make it plain to Christian people that they should not engage in them. Let this be the rule in choosing a life vocation: "Whether therefore ye eat, or drink, or whatsoever ye do, do all to the glory of God."

VIII. THE VICTORIOUS LIFE

For whatsoever is born of God overcometh the world: and this is the victory that overcometh the world, even our faith.—I Jno. 5:4.

We want to close this chapter with a few thoughts on the victorious life. According to the teaching of God's Word there is no need for the disciple of Christ to suffer defeat in his Christian life. God's promises are very definite that he may live a life of victory over self, sin, and Satan, right here in this life, and enjoy all the blessings that come from such a life. Here are a few points that may help us to attain to this blessed, victorious life.

1. Faith. Our Christian life must rest upon the structure of faith—faith in Christ as our Sin-bearer (Isa. 53:6), our Saviour (Heb. 7:25), our Lord and Master (Jno. 13:13), our Advocate with the Father (I Jno. 2:1). Notice the text quoted above. If we allow our faith to waver we cannot have victory.

2. A knowledge of God's Word. Unless we know what the Bible teaches and the promises that God has given to His people we do not have the equipment that we need to have victory in times of temptation, testing, and hardship. Send to the Mennonite Publishing House for tract entitled "Victory Verses." It will help you to a knowledge of what God's Word says about living a life of victory.

3. Prayer. We cannot hope to have victory unless we spend time in prayer. A snatch from a sacred

song says, "If you want victory, pray your way through." You cannot afford to neglect your prayer life. Eph. 6:18.

4. Full yielding to God. If we yield our lives one hundred per cent to God He can use us, bless us, and keep us in His will. This is one of the great secrets of the victorious life. Read Rom. 6:13.

5. Faithfulness in the use of all our talents, including money. We are simply stewards of all that we have and are. God expects us to use these gifts to His honor and glory. Let us not fail on this point.

6. A constant pressing on. If we keep going on in His service we are not very prone to be sidetracked and to leave the path of His will. Read Phil 3:13.

Let us look to God for grace to use these and all other helps to the victorious life. "And God is able to make all grace abound toward you; that ye, always having all sufficiency in all things, may abound to every good work" (II Cor. 9:8).

Chapter Six

ACTIVITY IN THE CHURCH

The Church on earth is the visible family of God. Members in this family, as in our natural families, are expected to be active workers and to help in the work or activities of the Church. We are saved not to live "on flowery beds of ease"; we are saved to serve. Every applicant should fully understand that each member of the Church should be a worker and a contributor, and not merely a hanger-on or one who aims to get the blessings and benefits of the Church without actively helping along in the work. In fact, in the work of the Church, as in many other things, we receive help and blessing in proportion as we give and serve. In natural growth a certain amount of exercise is necessary to insure proper development. Similarly we cannot expect to develop as we should in the spiritual life if we fail to work and exercise ourselves in spiritual matters.

In this chapter we are concerned mainly about the various public services of the Church. We need to have our private devotions and all the various forms of private worship and meditation upon God and His Word, but we also greatly need the help and strength that comes to us from united public worship. It is not intended that man should live and work alone. In all

lines of human activity we need companionship, and
the Bible teaches us very plainly the importance of
public or collective worship. To sing, pray, praise, to
be instructed in the Word, and in general to worship
together in the public meeting lifts us to spiritual
heights and brings us peculiar blessings that we cannot otherwise attain or receive. Here are a few Scriptures: "Where two or three are gathered together in
my name, there am I in the midst of them" (Matt. 18:
20); "Not forsaking the assembling of ourselves together: as the manner of some is; but exhorting one
another: and so much the more, as ye see the day
approaching" (Heb. 10:25). Subjects to be discussed
in this chapter are: Church Services; Sunday School;
Young People's Bible Meeting; Prayer Meeting; Bible
Study and Other Classes; Support of Missions and
Home Churches; Personal Work; Distributing Gospel Literature.

Church Services

**I was glad when they said unto me, Let us go into the
house of the Lord.—Psa. 122:1.**

Every church has its regular times for public services. They are held for the edification and strengthening of the body of the members. Every one who unites
with the Church should make it at once a practice of
attending every service that he possibly can. It is a
soul-chilling habit to attend church services only occa-
sionally. To become neglectful along this line means

that we deprive ourselves of one of the greatest helps and blessings in the Christian life. In Old Testament times God provided that His people should have a central place of worship. In the New Testament we find the believers at once meeting together for prayer, preaching, and worship. We find in the church service the highest type of Christian fellowship as we blend our hearts and voices in prayer and praise. In the sermon we receive instruction from God's Word from one who has been especially called of God for this purpose. If we prepare ourselves for this public worship by private devotion our hearts will be cleansed and open and ready to receive the blessings that God has for us in the church service. If we are in the spirit of worship we will be sure to receive a blessing.. If we are discouraged we will find help and strength; if we are sad we will find comfort; if we are withstanding temptations we will find strength for our need; if we are weak and weary in the struggle of life we will find new strength and zeal; and if we hunger we shall surely be filled.

"These public services are designed, therefore, and adapted to impart help to the sincere worshiper. No one can spend an hour in God's presence, looking up into His face and occupied with thoughts of Him to the exclusion of worldly thoughts, and not experience a cleansing of heart and a kindling of soul which will prove a great enriching of the life. All that is good in us receives quickening and a new impulse in such an atmosphere; all that is evil is checked and repressed." Let us not neglect to assemble together at the house of the Lord for worship, for here we shall find joy, blessing, and strength.

Sunday School

Study to shew thyself approved unto God, a workman that needeth not to be ashamed, rightly dividing the word of truth.—II Tim. 2:15.

The Sunday school is another of the public services of the Church, and it is especially designed to teach the Word. The young convert should make it a rule to attend this service conscientiously. Here he will find not only a chance to receive truth but to give as well. Every one in the class may take part in the interchange of opinions. All should attend, both young and old, but the young should especially take advantage of the opportunities which the Sunday school presents to become familiar with the Word of God in the time of life when learning is accomplished rather easily. The convert should hide God's Word in his mind and heart. Then he will be prepared for the hours of temptation that are sure to come. He will learn the principles of God's Word which will lead him in the right ways of life. He will be fitted for service in the Master's kingdom, because every acceptable workman for the Lord must have a working knowledge of the Bible.

The time may come when the convert will have an opportunity to teach a class, perhaps at first as a substitute, and later as a regular teacher. He should embrace these opportunities for service and perform them in the fear of the Lord and by His help. There are various special duties in Sunday-school work that some one must do. If called upon to do any of these the young Christian should accept the tasks and perform them as service that can be rendered for the Master who has done so much for him. The Sunday school is one of the great agencies of the Church for the training and preparation of workers in the Lord's service. Every member of the Church should attend and take part in the Sunday-school service in whatever way he has opportunity—either as pupil, teacher, or officer.

Young People's Bible Meeting

Let no man despise thy youth: but be thou an example of the believers . . . Till I come, give attendance to reading, to exhortation, to doctrine.—I Tim. 4:12, 13.

The young people's Bible meeting is a service of the Church which is designed to give the young people, and others also, an opportunity to learn to take part in public services. It is a sort of training school for young Christians. It is the aim of the young people's Bible meeting to give every member of the Church an opportunity to take part in the services, and every one who takes part receives training in gathering material for talks and in speaking in public. Not only is the young people's Bible meeting a fine training agency, but it is also the means of imparting valuable Scriptural information to those who attend as listeners. The topics are arranged to treat upon vital doctrinal, missionary, and Christian life subjects, and give a wider variety of teaching than is found in the Sunday school lessons. This is especially true of the doctrines of the Church, which are covered regularly during the course of a number of years. Every young convert should take full advantage of the opportunities of the young people's Bible meeting, both in the way of training for service and in receiving important Christian instruction.

Prayer Meeting

These all continued with one accord in prayer and supplication.—Acts 1:14.

The midweek prayer meeting fills another important place among the public services of the Church. It is an occasion when the Church meets together more particularly for prayer, although some form of instruction from the Word is also usually given. It is a meeting which refreshes our spiritual lives during the week, midway between the Sunday services. If tasks and difficulties and problems beset and oppress us it is refreshing to find our way to the house of God for renewed spiritual strength. Here often there is opportunity given for requests for special prayer. The young disciple of Christ should make it a point to attend the weekly church prayer meeting and to take part in the period open for prayers by the audience.

Bible Study and Other Classes

They received the word with all readiness of mind, and searched the scriptures daily, whether those things were so.—Acts 17:11.

Nearly every congregation at some time or other arranges for special classes for the young people. These may be classes in Bible Study, Mission Study, Teacher Training, Personal Work, or some other systematic study. Every young Christian should avail himself of every such opportunity for Christian instruction and training.

Support of Missions and Home Churches

For even in Thessalonica ye sent once and again unto my necessity.—Phil. 4:16.

The young convert should train himself to support every activity of the Church by prayer, service, and financial help. Special opportunities come to Christian people to support organized mission work, both at home and abroad. Each disciple should form the habit of praying for the varied church activities, for this is one of the most valuable ways of giving support. Pray for the missionaries whom you know, for the work at the various stations, for the great numbers of unsaved people. As you have opportunity be sure to give your hearty financial support to the mission cause. The Church needs your help to carry on this great work of carrying the Gospel to every creature. As opportunities come your way you should not hesitate to help along in mission work. Perhaps you can teach in a mission Sunday school somewhere near your home community or perform some other helpful service.

Do not neglect to support your home church, however. Remember your church leaders and brethren and sisters in prayer, and especially intercede for the weak ones in the faith and those who are unsaved. Do not neglect your financial obligations to the home church. There are expenses to be met in taking care of the local work. Be sure to do your share. The Church brings you many blessings, and these blessings will multiply as you help along in the work in whatever way you can.

Personal Work

And Philip ran thither to him.—Acts 8:30.

One of the last words of Jesus to His disciples was that they should be witnesses for Him. We can be witnesses in many ways, quite a number of which have been referred to in preceding parts of this book. But one of the most effective ways of testifying for Jesus is in personal work. As we meet people in our daily life and work we have the blessed privilege of telling them about Jesus and His power to save. Many souls have been won for Christ in this way; in fact this is said to be the most effective means of soul-winning. Jesus used this method, as well as the apostles. The young Christian will find that as he testifies for

Jesus in his personal contacts with people he will be strengthened in the faith, will receive blessings in his own life, and will be the means of bringing spiritual help and blessing to others.

Distributing Gospel Literature

Blessed are ye that sow beside all waters.—Isa. 32:20.

This is another effective way of witnessing for Jesus and helping along in the work of the Church. The world today is flooded with literature. Most of this has no spiritual value whatever, and much is positively harmful. It is part of the work of the Church to supply sound Christian literature and thus help to spread the Gospel through the printed page. A good habit for the Christian to form is to have some good Gospel tracts or papers with him to give to people whom he meets in his work or in travel. Inexpensive Gospels and other Scripture portions may readily be obtained. These are fine to distribute in hospitals. jails, or in visitation work among the sick or others. Learn to witness for Jesus wherever you are.

Chapter Seven

THE BLESSEDNESS OF THE CHRISTIAN LIFE

The Christian life is one of much blessing in this life, and in addition to this present blessedness the follower of Christ has the glorious hope of looking forward to the return of his Lord and to spending eternity with Him in heaven.

Present Rewards and Blessings

Who hath blessed us with all spiritual blessings in heavenly places in Christ.—Eph. 1:3.

Any one who has whole-heartedly entered the Christian life has at once experienced some rich blessings. As the sinner feels his sins forgiven through the blood of Christ, peace and joy fills his heart to an extent that he has never experienced before. This is the direct result of salvation. And it is the will of Christ that this joy and peace in increasing fullness shall go with him all through his life. "Peace I leave with you, my peace I give unto you" (Jno. 14:27). "These things have I spoken unto you, that my joy might remain in you, and that your joy might be full" (Jno. 15:11). Trials and difficulties the Christian undoubtedly will have, but through them all he can "rejoice with joy unspeakable and full of glory" (I Pet. 1:8).

To be freed from the bondage of sin and Satan is a great reward in itself. The one who lives in sin is a slave to his evil desires and passions and often becomes bound with vile habits that waste body and mind. From these and many other evils the true Christian enjoys the blessing of freedom, and he can rejoice with Paul in the thought that "there is therefore now no condemnation to them which are in Christ Jesus, who walk not after the flesh, but after the Spirit. For the law of the Spirit of life in Christ Jesus hath made me free from the law of sin and death" (Rom. 8:1, 2).

Then again the Christian has rich joys and rewards in service even in this life. He has the consciousness that his labor is not in vain in the Lord (I Cor. 15:58), and many times he can see at least some of the results of his work as souls confess Christ or grow and develop into faithful Christian workers through his teaching and encouragement or other efforts. And just to serve the One who loved us and gave Himself for us is indeed a great joy and satisfaction in itself. Then the blessed association and fellowship with others who are engaged in the same service is also an inestimable blessing. The home, the farm, the office, the shop, all places where we live and serve, are made more hallowed and blessed because we are followers of Christ. And then as we have His presence and that of His Holy Spirit with us from day to day, we can well say that "it pays to serve

Jesus" every day in this life, although we look also for a blessed life of eternal joy in the future.

The Blessed Hope

Looking for that blessed hope, and the glorious appearing of the great God and our Saviour Jesus Christ.— Tit. 2:13.

The Bible teaches very plainly that our Lord Jesus Christ shall return from heaven in like manner as He went to heaven. In I Thess. 4:13-18 we are told that when He shall come from heaven "with a shout, with the voice of the archangel, and with the trump of God," the believers, both living and dead, will be caught up to meet Him in the air, to be with Him forever. In the text quoted above, the second coming of our Lord is referred to as "that blessed hope," and in this sense it has become very dear to the heart of the true Christian. This event is indeed something to hope for and to look forward to, for when that blessed time shall come the sorrows and toils of earth will all be over and we shall from thenceforth enjoy the personal presence of our Lord as we dwell with Him through the eternal ages.

Every Christian should keep this hope constantly before him. He should continually watch and wait for the return of his Lord. Not only will this hope be a source of joy and blessing to him, but it will help to make his life of the character that it should be. "Every man that hath this hope in him purifieth himself, even as he is pure" (I Jno. 3:3). As we think of the fact that Jesus may come at any time we will be diligent in keeping our lives pure so that we will always be ready to meet Him. Mark expresses it like this: "Take ye heed, watch and pray: for ye know not when the time is" (13:33). Hence, as we watch and pray and hope for His return we deny ungodliness and set our affections on heavenly things. The hope for His imminent return also spurs us on to work diligently for the salvation of the lost while we may. The young Christian should at once learn both to love and to look for "that blessed hope" of the return of our Lord to receive His people to Himself.

The Eternal Home

And he . . . shewed me that great city, the holy Jerusalem.—Rev. 21:10.

As Christians we should serve the Lord because of our love for Him who did so much for us. Yet it is not wrong to keep in mind the reward of the faithful. We have already spoke of the many rewards and blessings that come to the Christian in this life. Now we want to think of the rewards that come to us in heaven. Jesus said of those who suffer persecution for His sake: "Rejoice, and be exceeding glad; for great is your reward in heaven" (Matt. 5:12). In the last chapter of the Bible we read these words: "Behold, I come quickly; and my reward is with me, to give every man according as his work shall be" (Rev. 22:12). And so we see that our blessed Lord will reward every one of us according to the work that we do here upon earth.

We do not know what all these rewards will comprise, but we have glimpses which show us some of the glory that He has prepared for His faithful disciples. We shall be transformed; these bodies of humiliation will be like His own glorious body; and we shall be like Him and see Him as He is. We shall have a share in the city of gold, in the many mansions that He has prepared. We shall join in the chorus of praise which all the redeemed of all ages shall sing around the great white throne of God and His Son. Words cannot begin to describe the glorious rewards of the faithful in the eternal home of the blest. Let us, then, press on faithfully in the work which we have begun as new disciples of our Lord, and we shall be blest above all that we can ask or think, both in this world and in the world to come.

Chapter Eight

THE ADMINISTRATION OF BAPTISM

(This chapter is taken from the Minister's Manual for the Mennonite Church, compiled by J. F. Funk, and published by the Mennonite Publishing House, Scottdale, Pa. At some time during the instruction, preferably at the last meeting for that purpose, the applicant should be made familiar with the actual procedure of the administration of the baptismal ceremony.)

When any person, by the grace of God, has come to a saving knowledge of the truth, and desires to enter into a covenant with God to be baptized and received into church membership, he should make known his desire to the bishop or minister, or to any member of the Church, who may inform the minister. The bishop or minister then inquires of the applicant whether he believes that his desire to live a better life is a call from God to the saving of his soul; whether he realizes that he himself is not able to do any part of the saving work, and that it is impossible for him of his own will to continue faithful in the good work begun in his heart; whether he believes that God, of His own grace and power, will, upon true repentance, forgive him his sins, give him a new heart, adopt him into the family of God, and receive him into the fellowship of the saints. Also whether he is willing to submit himself to the Gospel of Jesus Christ and His nonresistant doctrine, in all things to be advised and instructed by the Word of God; whether he is at peace with his neighbor and fellow men generally, so far as is possible, and whether he is connected with any secret society, or ıs in any other way living contrary to the teachings of the Gospel as we interpret it, and if so, whether he is willing unconditionally to withdraw from any such secret organization, and in every respect to renounce all the errors of his former life. If the applicant gives satisfactory evidence that he is prompted by the Spirit of God, and is willing to conform to the requirements of the Gospel, the bishop or minister publishes the request before the congregation, and admonishes the members to observe the walk and conduct of the applicant, to show him a good example in a pious spiritual life, and to pray for him.

The subject or subjects (if more than one) for baptism should then be well instructed in the doctrines of repentance, forgiveness of sins, regeneration, the life of God in the soul, the ordinances to be observed, the restrictions which the Gospel places upon the Christian, and the rules of church government. The meetings for this purpose may be held at the meetinghouse or at some other convenient place, on the afternoon of each meeting day, or any other appropriate time and place may be selected. The minister should give such instructions on the above-mentioned subjects and others, as he may consider suitable and necessary. The converts should be instructed to read and study carefully the eighteen articles of our Confession of faith, and the minister should make it his duty to see that they understand them. They should also be made acquainted with the rules and requirements of the Church, as well as the duties which church membership imposes upon them, and the privileges it bestows.

The object of these instructions is to edify and confirm the subjects for baptism in their faith, and encourage them to persevere in the right way. All applicants for baptism and admission into the Church should be able to give satisfactory evidence that they have truly repented of their sins, and have found peace in their souls through faith in Jesus Christ, and that they have passed from death unto life.

At least three or four of these meetings should be held before baptism. In some places they are held much oftener. These should be opened and closed with prayer, and if practicable, with the singing of a hymn. In many places the instruction meetings are held publicly, the members and the congregation in general being present, which is appropriate and profitable for both the members and the unconverted.

In some localities before baptism is administered a counsel of the Church is held for the purpose of as-

certaining whether there is any Scriptural reason to
prevent the admission of any of the applicants into
the Church. If no cause is found, they are requested
to meet again on the day preceding baptism, upon
which occasion the eighteen articles of the Confession
are read to them and explained, and they are asked
whether they believe in and fully agree with these doctrines. If they answer in the affirmative, they are ex-
horted to stand firmly, and be faithful in the commandments of God, and to continue in good works
unto the end.

In other places the names of the applicants are
simply published in the meeting, and if no objection
is presented, and the candidates have been sufficiently
instructed, either publicly or privately, the time for
baptism is appointed, and the exercises are proceeded
with as follows:

After singing a hymn the minister or deacon may
appropriately read John 1:1-36. After the usual open-
ing services and prayer the bishop or another minister
takes an appropriate text and preaches a discourse
from it (observing not to preach too long).

He then descends from the desk, and says to the
congregation: "When our dear Lord and Saviour Jesus
Christ gave His last commission to His disciples He
said, 'All power is given unto me in heaven and in
earth. Go ye therefore, and teach all nations, baptizing them in the name of the Father, and of the Son,
and of the Holy Ghost: teaching them to observe all

things whatsoever I have commanded you.' And again, 'Go ye into all the world, and preach the gospel to every creature. He that believeth and is baptized shall be saved; but he that believeth not shall be damned.' In accordance with these declarations of the Word of God, these dear souls have presented themselves before us for the purpose of being baptized, and thus making a covenant with God, and being received into the communion and fellowship of the Church.

"They have been instructed in the doctrines of the Gospel and in the ordinances and requirements of the Church, and have given evidence that they are prompted in their purpose by the Spirit of God, that they are willing to forsake sin and the world, to consecrate themselves to the service of God, and from henceforth to be the disciples and followers of Christ. As we now are witnesses of these solemn exercises, let each one of us remember our own covenant and pray that the solemn promises which shall be made here today before God and this congregation, may be made in all sincerity, and that God may bless and establish these dear souls in His grace, that they may be strong in the Lord, zealous in good works, ornaments in the Christian profession, shining lights in the world, and faithful in all things unto the end. And as there is joy in heaven over one sinner that repenteth, so let our hearts rejoice that God has led these precious souls to turn from their former ways and come into the fold of Christ. As we thus rejoice let

us likewise pray that God may lead yet many more
to follow their good example. Amen."

Addressing the applicants, the minister says: "And
now if it is still your desire to be baptized and received
into church fellowship, you will arise."

He then addresses to the applicants the following questions:

1. "Do you believe in one true, eternal, and al-
mighty God, who is the Creator and Preserver of all
visible and invisible things?"

Answer: "I do."

2. "Do you believe in Jesus Christ, as the only
begotten Son of God, that He is the only Saviour of
mankind, that He died upon the cross, and gave Himself a ransom for our sins, that through Him we might
have eternal life?"

Answer: "I do."

3. "Do you believe in the Holy Ghost which
proceedeth from the Father and the Son; that He is
an abiding Comforter, sanctifies the hearts of men, and
guides them into all truth?"

Answer: "I do."

(Note.—The foregoing questions are, by some,
combined in one; but it is better to ask them separate-
ly, in order that they may be better understood.)

4. "Are you truly sorry for your past sins, and
are you willing to renounce Satan, the world, and all

works of darkness, and your own carnal will and sinful desires?"

Answer "I am."

5. "Do you promise by the grace of God, and the aid of the Holy Spirit, to submit yourself to Christ and His Word, and faithfully to abide in the same until death?"

Answer: "I do."

After these questions have been asked and answered affirmatively the minister and the subjects for baptism kneel, while the congregation stands, and the minister prays for God's blessing upon them, that they may have grace to remain steadfast and be faithful to the end in the promises they have made.

After prayer the minister arises, while the subjects for baptism remain kneeling. The deacon or some other brother now brings a vessel with water, and the minister, laying his hands upon the head of the subject for baptism, says,

"Upon the confession of thy faith, which thou hast made before God and these witnesses (he now with both hands takes a quantity of water from the vessel and pours it upon the head of the applicant), I baptize thee with water, in the name of the Father, and of the Son, and of the Holy Ghost."*

---

* Some, instead of "Which thou hast made before God and these witnesses," say, "Repentance and sorrow for thy sins," etc.

After all the applicants are thus baptized, the minister returns to the one first baptized, and taking him by the hand says:

"In the name of Christ and His Church I give you my hand. Arise! And as Christ was raised up by the glory of the Father, even so thou also shalt walk in newness of life, and as long as thou art faithful and abidest in the doctrine of His Word, thou art His disciple indeed, and shalt be acknowledged as a member of the body of Christ, and a brother (or sister) in the Church." He then gives him the kiss of peace and says: "The Lord bless thee and keep thee. Amen."

In the same manner he also raises the female converts, and the wife of the minister or deacon, or any sister in the Church, gives them the kiss of peace, and thus receives them into the fellowship of the Church.

The minister now takes his place again at the desk, and gives such further instruction as he may deem necessary, after which the services are closed in the usual manner.

Receiving Members from Other Denominations

If any person who has been connected with another denomination, and having been baptized upon the confession of his faith,* wishes to unite with the Church, he is not rebaptized, unless he desires it, but

---

* Persons who were baptized in their infancy can not be received into the Church without being rebaptized.

is taught the doctrines of the Bible, and the rules of order as we believe and practice them. If he agrees with these, and the Church has no cause against him the minister, in the presence of the whole congregation, asks him the following questions:

"Do you confess that you are of the same mind with us in the doctrines and rules of the Church; and do you promise to remain faithful and obedient in the same until death?" If he answers this affirmatively the minister takes him by the hand saying:

"Upon this confession which thou hast made before God and these witnesses, thou shalt be acknowledged as a brother (or sister) in the Church: and as long as thou art faithful and abidest in the doctrine of His Word, thou art His disciple indeed." The kiss of peace is then given, and he says: "The Lord bless thee and keep thee. Amen."

Some prefer the following more complete form:

"Do you acknowledge and confess that you agree and are of one mind with us in the doctrines and faith of the Mennonite Church, and that you acknowledge and accept them as in accordance with the teachings of the Gospel; and do you promise by the grace of God and the aid of His Holy Spirit to submit yourself to them, and also to her rules of order and forms of worship, and to remain faithful and obedient in the same until death?"

Answer: "I do."

"Then in the name of Jesus Christ and His Church I give thee my hand, and welcome thee to the communion and fellowship of this Church and congregation and to the Church in general, and as long as thou **art faithful and abidest in the doctrine of His Word,** thou art His disciple indeed, and shalt be acknowledged as a member of the body of Christ and a brother (or sister) in the Church."

The minister then gives the usual salutation and says:

"The Lord bless thee and keep thee. Amen."

Frequently applicants prefer to be baptized in the water. In this case the questions are sometimes asked, and the prayer offered in the house. The services here may be closed by the singing of a hymn before proceeding to the water. Here the minister, standing with the converts near the water, surrounded by the congregation, reads Acts 8:35-39, or some other short and appropriate Scripture. He may also add, as circumstances may suggest, a few words of comment, or admonition, or the congregation may sing a hymn. The minister then leads the applicants, one or two at a time, into the water, where the applicants kneel and the minister takes up water with both hands, pours it on their heads, and proceeds further as described above.